**Architectural Guide
Helsinki**

For Nina

Architectural Guide
Helsinki

Ulf Meyer

With additional contributions from Douglas Gordon,
Laura Kolbe und Heikki Mäntymäki

DOM publishers

Content

The eastern and western spirit of Helsinki *Laura Kolbe* 16
Recycling area at the polar circle *Douglas Gordon, Heikki Mäntymäki* 22
Maps 162
Architects 172
Directory 173
Authors 175

Chapter 1: Inner Center, from page 26

Chapter 2: Around the Center, from page 68

Chapter 3: Northwest, from page 90

Chapter 4: East, from page 112

Chapter 5: Vantaa / Espoo, from page 142

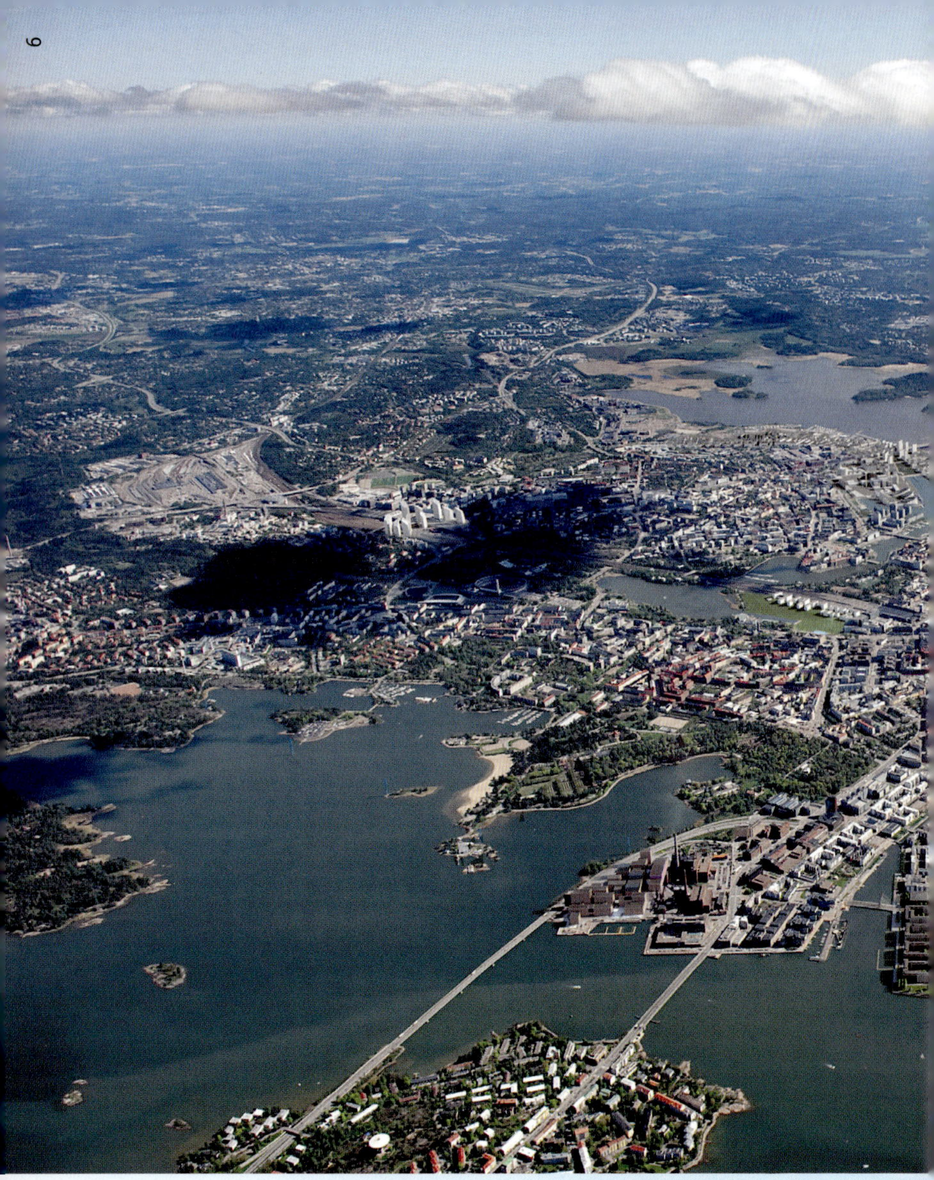

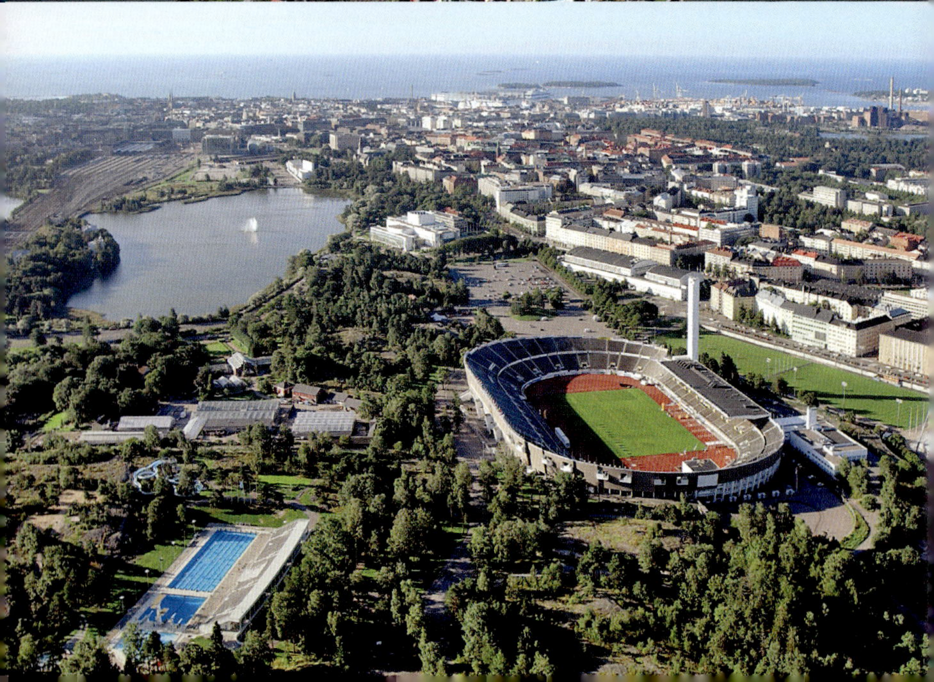

7

A
MEILAHTI
MEJLANS
MEILAHDEN URHEILUPUISTO
MEJLANS IDROTTSPARK
SÄDEHOITOKLINIKKA
STRÅLBEHANDLINGSKLINIKEN
SILMÄTAUTIEN KLINIKKA
KLINIKEN FÖR ÖGONSJUKDOMAR
NAISTENKLINIKKA
KVINNOKLINIKEN
MEILAHDEN SAIRAALA
MEJLANS SJUKHUS
LASTEN JA NUORTEN SAIRAALA
BARN OCH UNGDOMSSJUKHUSET
LASTENLINNAN SAIRAALA
BARNETS BORGS SJUKHUS
Haartmaninkatu
Haartmansgatan
Stenbäckinkatu
Stenbäcksgatan
Topeliuksenkatu
Paciuksenkatu
Paciusgatan
Linnankoskigatan
Arvo Ylpön puisto
Mikael Lybeckin katu
Mikael Lybecks gata
084
079
081
Maila Talvion puisto
Humallahdenpuisto
Hummelviksparken
Humallahti
Hummelviken
Kesäranta
Merikannontie
Råholmsvägen
Rajasaarentie
Rajasaari
Råholmen
Humalluodot
Hummelgrunden
Sibeliuksen puisto
Sibeliusparken
Mechelininkatu
Kesäkatu
Sommargatan
SOUTUSTADION
RODDSTADION
Toivo Kuulan puisto
Toivo Kuulas park
Seurasaarenselkä
Fölisöfjärden
Taivallahti
Edesviken
Taivalsaari
Edesholmen
Taivalluoto
Edesgrundet
Taivallahden verkkopallokenttä
Edesvikens tennisplaner
Juutalainen hautausmaa
Judiska begravningsplatsen
Hietaranta
Sandstrand
Hietaniemen uurnalehto
Sandudds urnlund
Hietakannas
Sandnäs
KREMATORIOKAPPELI
KREMATORIEKAPELLET
Hietaniemi
Sandudd
HIETANIEMEN KAPPELI
SANDUDDS KAPELL
Uusi Luterilainen hautausmaa
Nya Lutherska begravningsplatsen
SANKARIHAUDAT
HJÄLTEGRAVARNA
Hietaniemen hautausmaa
Sandudds kyrkogård
Sanduddsgatan
Ourit
Órarna
Hietaniemenkarit
Sanduddsgrunden
Lapinlahti
Lappviken
Lapinniemi
Lappudden

101
099
097
082
080
076
062
069
061
063
067
058
059
068
071
060
070
055
054
017
024
020
019
009
018
047
046
006
050
FINNAIR STADIUM
JÄÄHALLI ISHALLEN
URHEILUMUSEO IDROTTSMUSEET
OLYMPIASTADION
STADIONIN TORNI STADIONTORNET
UIMASTADION SIMSTADION
KAUPUNGIN TALVIPUUTARHA STADENS VINTERTRÄDGÅRD
LINNANMÄEN HUVIPUISTO BORGBACKENS NÖJESPARK
Linnanmäki Borgbacken
Alppipuisto Alpparken
DIAKONISSALAITOS DIAKONISSANSTALTEN
Helsinginkatu
Mäntymäenkenttä Tallbacksfältet
Mäntymäki Tallbacka
TÖÖLÖN KISAHALLI TÖLÖ SPORTHALL
Eino Leinon katu
Sibeliuksenkatu
Suomen Kansallisooppera Finska Nationalopera
Töölönlahti Tölöviken
TÖÖLÖN SAIRAALA TÖLÖ SJUKHUS
Hesperian puisto Hesperiaparken
Hakasalmen puisto Hagasunds park
Pohjoinen Hesperiankatu
Runeberginkatu
Mannerheimintie
FINLANDIA-TALO FINLANDIA-HUSET
SUOMEN KANSALLISMUSEO FINLANDS NATIONALMUSEUM
HAKASALMEN HUVILA VILLA HAGASUND
Auroran kenttä
MUSIIKKITALO MUSIKHUSET
Museokatu
Museon puisto Museiparken
Eduskuntapuisto
EDUSKUNTATALO RIKSDAGSHUSET
KIASMA NYKYTAITEEN MUSEO
Arkadiankatu
Arkadiagatan
LUONNONTIETEELLINEN MUSEO NATURHISTORISKA MUSEET
TAIDEHALLI KONSTHALLEN
KAUPPAKORKEAKOULU
Postikatu
POSTITALO POSTHUSET
HOTELLIKESKUS HOTELLCENTRALEN
LASIPALATSI GLASPALATSET
LINJA-AUTOASEMA BUSSSTATION
Narinkka
Kaivokatu
Simonkatu
YLIOPPILASTALO STUDENTHUSET
TAIDEMUSEO KONSTMUSEUM
Kolmen sepän aukio
TENNISPALATSI
Urho Kekkosen katu
Hietaniemenkatu
Perhonkatu
Temppeliaukion kirkko
Mika Waltarin puisto
Apollonkatu
Museigatan
Fredrikinkatu
Töölöntori Tölötorg
Sandelsinkatu

B

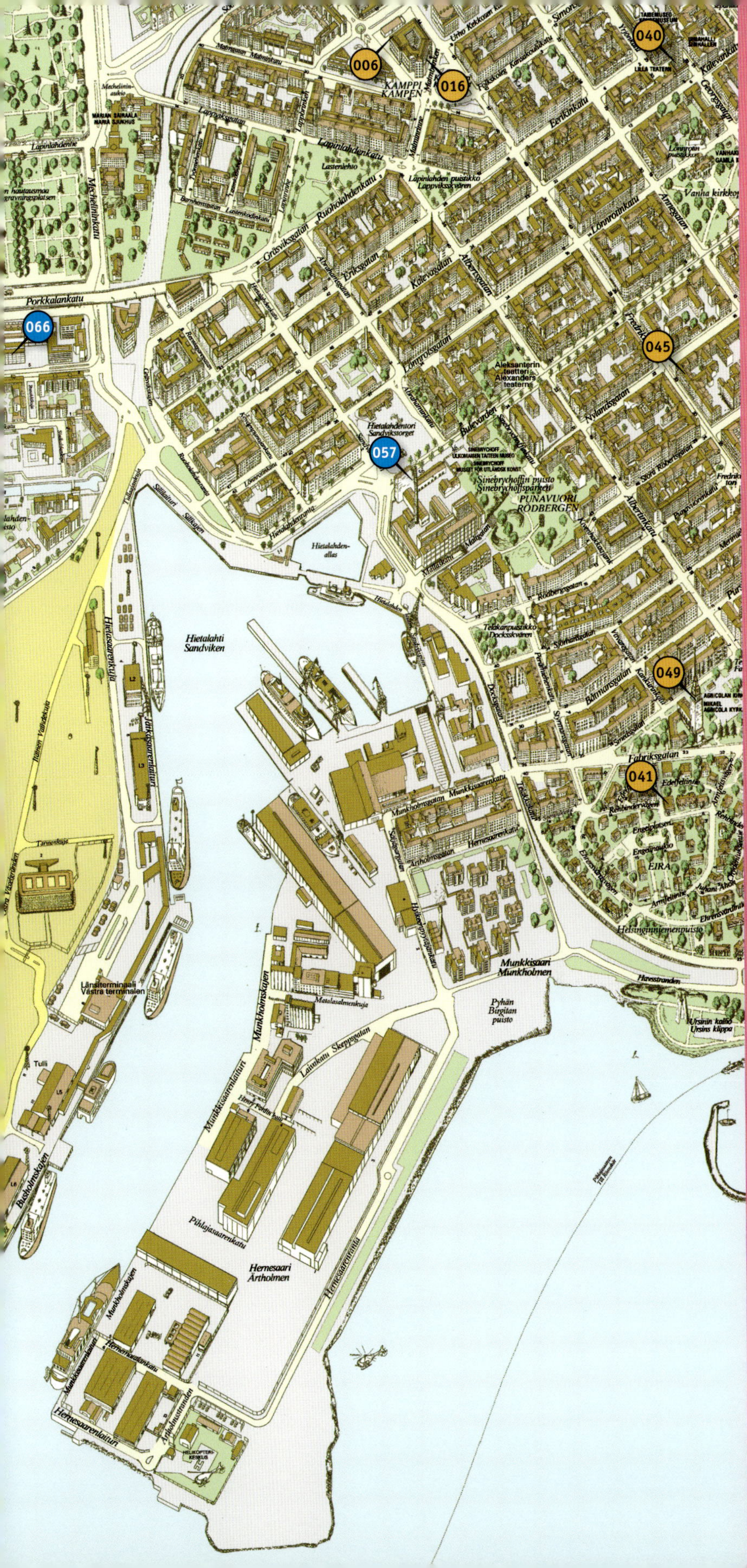

006
016
040
066
045
057
049
041
KAMPPI
KAMPEN
Porkkalankatu
Lapinlahdenkatu
Ruoholahdenkatu
Lönnrotinkatu
Albertinkatu
Hietalahdentori
Sandvikstorget
Aleksanterin teatteri
Alexanders teatern
Sinebrychoffin puisto
Sinebrychoffsparken
PUNAVUORI
RÖDBERGEN
Hietalahden-
allas
Hietalahti
Sandviken
Fabriksgatan
EIRA
Helsinginniemenpuisto
Munkkisaari
Munkholmen
Pyhän
Birgitan
puisto
Ursinin kallio
Ursins klippa
Länsiterminaali
Västra terminalen
Tulli
Hernesaari
Ärtholmen

C

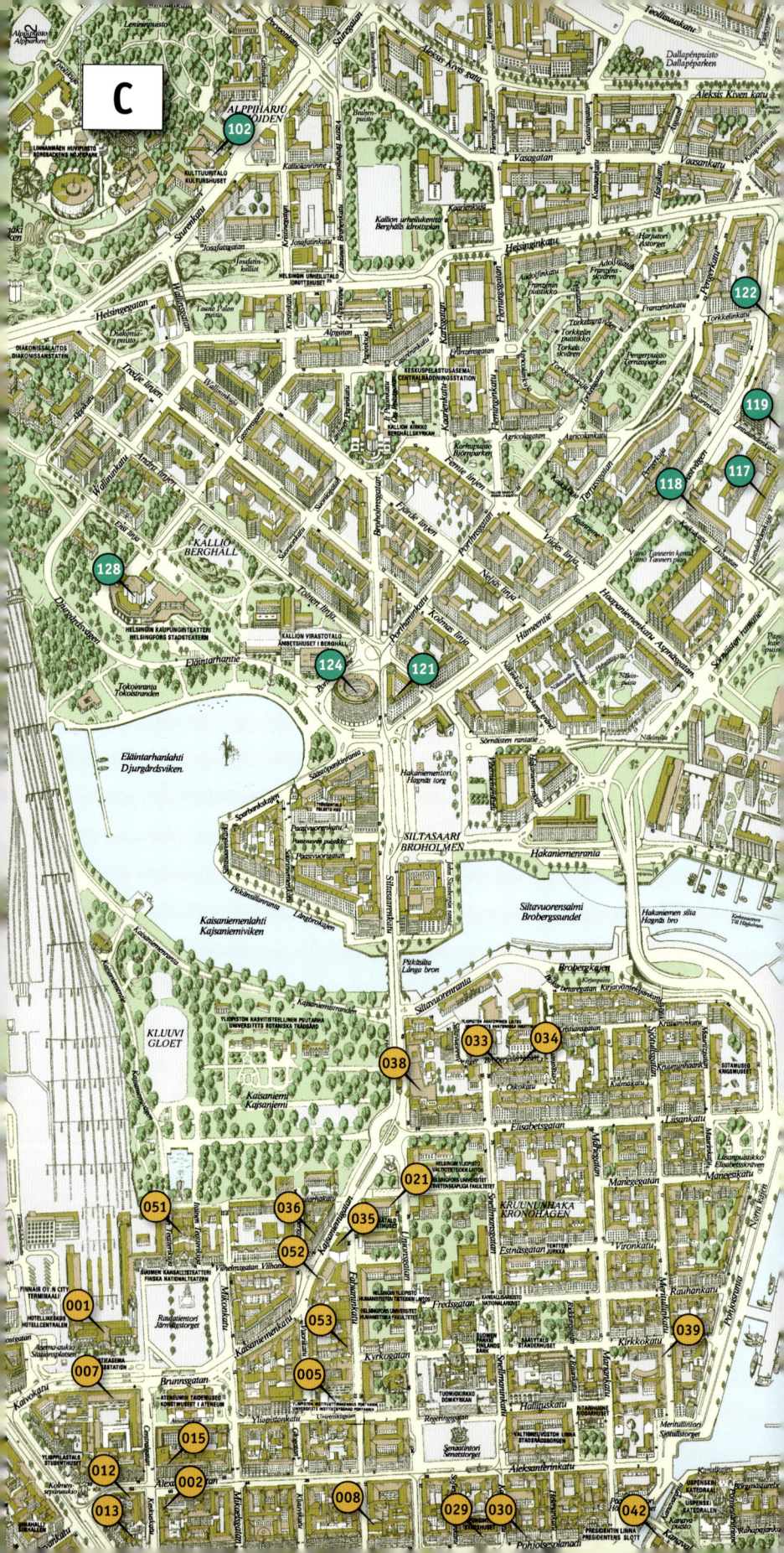

Kalasatama

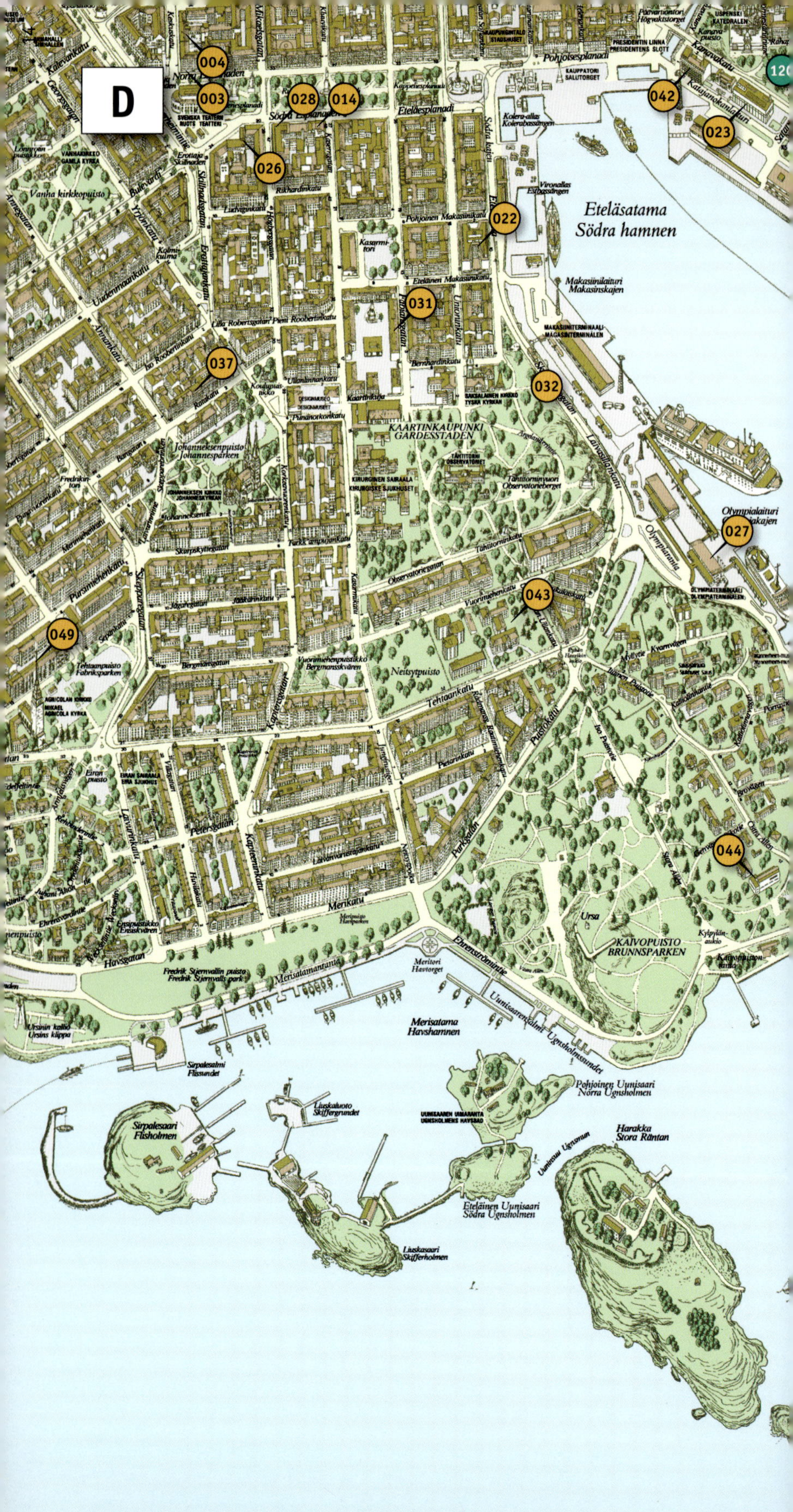

© Kaupunkimittausosasto, Helsinki

15

010
011
025
048

Katajanokka
Skatudden

Risteilylaituri

Katajanokanluoto
Skatakobben

Valkosaarensalmi
Blekholmssundet

Ryssäsaari
Ryssholmen

Pikkuluoto
Lilläppan

Pormestarinhepo
Borgmästarhästen

Limppu
Limpan

Pormestarinluodot
Borgmästargrunden

Särkkä
Långören

Pikku-Musta
Lilla Östersvartö

Merisotakoulu
Sjökrigsskolan
B.Stiernkrook
B.Stenberg
B.Scheffer

LAUTTALAITURI
FÄRJA

NEUVONTA
INFORMATION

Löwenhjelm

Suomenlinna
Sveaborg

Kruununlinna
Kronverket Ehrensv.

Varvilahti
Varvviken

The eastern and western spirit of Helsinki

Laura Kolbe

Every capital city has its own topography, visual landmarks, main monument, symbol and story. They usually become a part of the urban image and cultural narrative, giving a cultural orientation to the city. When walking through Helsinki one soon notices the lack of old European landmarks. There is no historic urban core, old town or remains of a fortress or medieval city center, as in other capital cities along the Baltic Sea or in Scandinavia. On the contrary, Helsinki's urban story is based on its modern capital city status and on its location by the sea on the Gulf of Finland.

Helsinki is not an old bourgeois town or commercial melting pot. It came about as the result of royal and imperial politics. The city's history is closely connected with the powers around the Baltic. Helsinki's location on the sea, between East and West, has been an advantage for the city. Helsinki is a blue and white city. The Vantaa River, the waterfront areas, the bays, shores and coastline, as well as being on the isthmus have shaped its historical development. The building of the maritime fortification of Suomenlinna, or Sveaborg, proudly called the "Gibraltar of the North", began in 1748, and the fortress marked an upswing in the modest economy of Helsinki. The city still opens up from the sea, and is best seen from ship approaching the harbor. The classical, historical silhouette of the city, its two great cathedrals (Lutheran and Orthodox) and its low-profile, appearing to rise directly from the sea, white, classical and horizontal. The sea has played a key role in shaping the city, a heritage preserved in Helsinki's symbols. The coat of arms (1640) shows a boat and waves, indicating the medieval settlement history and closeness to the sea.

The center—Senate and Market Square—are close to the sea. The neo-classical waterfront facade is a well known urban symbol of the city. With the industrialization, land was reclaimed from the sea for harbors and dockyards. For a long time, the easiest approach to Helsinki was by sea. Today the maritime silhouette is made up of ferries, motor and sailing boats, cruise- and passengerships and ice-breakers. The old harbor

South Harbour (1893) and the Senate Square; bird's eye (2011)

17

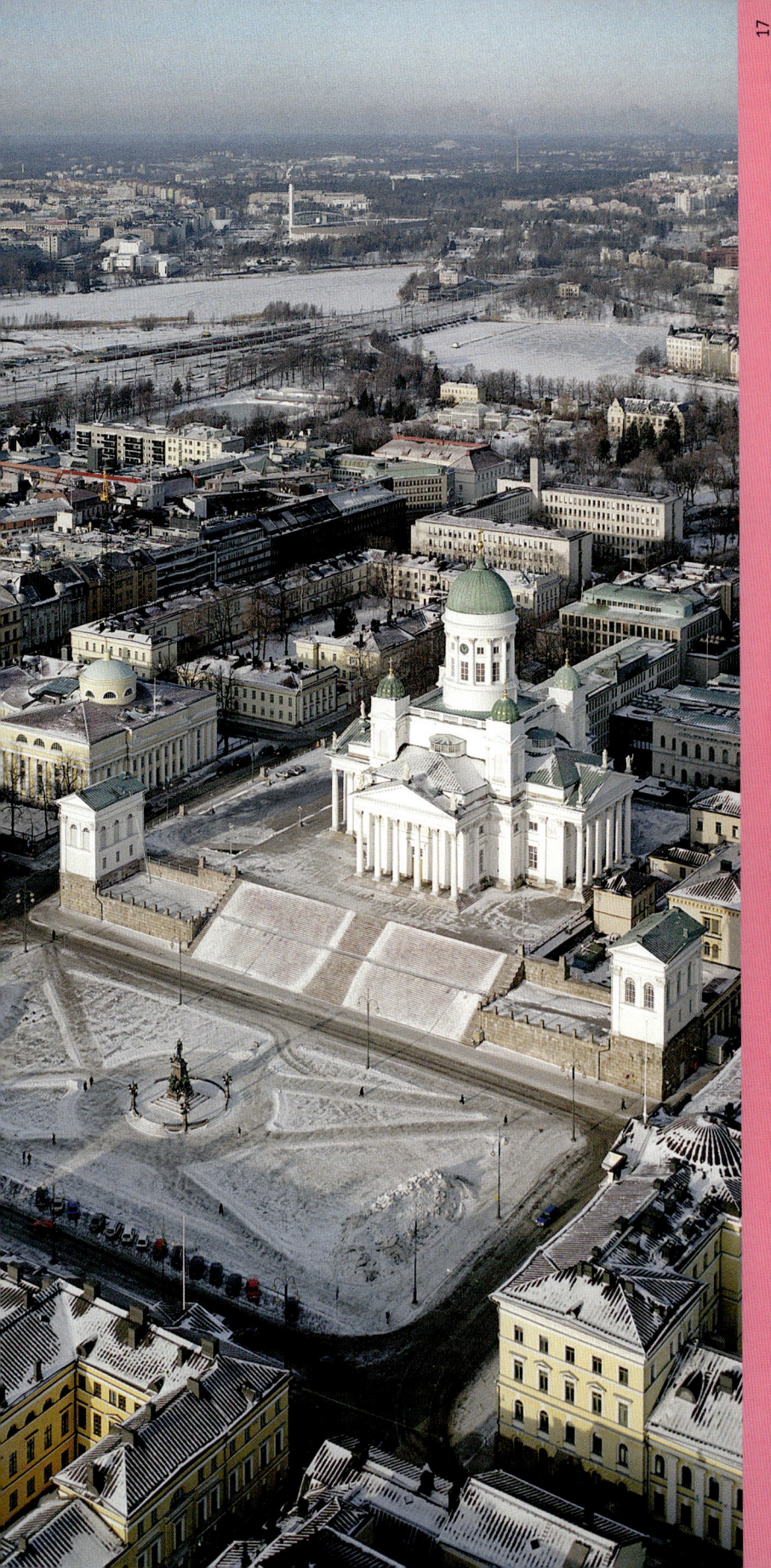

Uspenski Cathedral (1868) by Russian architect Alexey Gornostaev

and industrial areas along the shore are being turned into attractive residential neighborhoods. Suburban planning has also moved along the coast line; oceanfronts have become desirable residential and recreational areas. The Vuosaari harbor and other new urban waterfront projects will reinforce Helsinki's image as a maritime city.

Helsinki's development is similar to that of other medium-sized capitals in Central and Eastern Europe. An administrative tradition of civil servant rule, an industrial structure geared towards agriculture, a lack of capital and a slow industrial and logistical take-off caused true urbanization to get off to a late start. An identity balanced between western and eastern influences has dominated the city's history. In Helsinki, industrial development has been neither rapid nor massive. In the family of European capital cities, Helsinki is rather young. The years 1550, 1640, 1812, 1917, 1952 and 1975 are milestones in Helsinki's history. Unlike many other European cities, Helsinki has a clear foundation date – actually two.

Helsinki (Swedish "Helsingfors") was established in 1550 by the Swedish king Gustavus I. Vasa to compete with old Hanseatic Tallinn on the opposite side of the Gulf of Finland. This dream never became a reality. Numerous fires, wars between Russia and Sweden, occupations, plagues and scarcity had slowed the evolution of the town. Nor did the town's relocation by Queen Christina of Sweden in 1640 to today's location of central Helsinki on the isthmus, improve the situation. Helsinki remained a medium-sized Swedish coastal town. Today, the bilingualism of Finnish and Swedish still marks the "western" and Swedish influence.

The second founding date forms a more essential part of the town's identity. In 1812, Helsinki was raised to the capital of Finland by decree of the Russian Zsar Alexander I. Finland had been separated from Sweden in the wake of the great wars in Europe, and annexed to the Russian Empire as a Grand Duchy. Finland's position was connected to St. Petersburg – at that time the capital of Russia and a center of power on the Baltic Sea rim, only 300 kilometers east of Helsinki. Inaugural words for the new capital were pronounced by the Russian Zsar.

Becoming an Imperial Russian city having been a Royal Swedish town implied a rise in status. In 1812, the Russian Zsar appointed Helsinki's first town planning authority. This marked a change of policy, since the old town had grown slowly and without any city plan. The new town plan, confirmed by the Emperor in 1817, showed the classical and regular town planning ideal of European towns. The city's identity as a center of provincial government was underscored by the architecturally and ideologically apt

Lutheran Cathedral (1852) by German architect Carl Ludwig Engel

Imperial style. Construction began in 1816, when the Reconstruction Committee hired Berlin-born architect Carl Ludwig Engel. Helsinki became a means of expression for Russian imperial power. Rapidly, on an almost virgin site, a new city was built. From the rocky ground there sprang up barracks, churches, administrative buildings, a university with its beautiful library, observatory, greenhouse and clinic. Within decades Helsinki was able to compete in beauty with the most prominent European capitals. The regular and hierarchical neoclassicism conveyed a message of political conservatism, continuity, order and stability.

The investments of the central power heavily influenced the development of the Helsinki since the early decades of 19th century. After the opening of railway connections in 1864 Helsinki become the cultural and political center of the country, a real capital. The driving force of modernization consisted of cadres and civil servants who had received a 19th century-education. The most important modernist and "western" phase occured in 1875–1914. The Imperial city became a municipality, with a local government, planning its local infrastructure. Seen in terms of cultural and political geography, Helsinki's location on the Baltic Sea, between East and West, has been an advantage for the city. The "Golden Age" of Helsinki is the period before the Word War I. Helsinki had become the cultural, intellectual and political center of the country, a real capital and small metropolis. The general increase in wealth expressed itself a significant increase in planning and construction projects.

In line with European models, the planning of the city emphasized technological modernity, aesthetic aspects and urban intimacy: Jugendstil as befitted the tasty of the city's new middle class. Urban planning shifted from engineers to architects. In the first decades of the 20th century several private garden suburbs were built outside Helsinki, like Kulosaari, Haaga, Munkkiniemi, Pukinmäki and Huopalahti. These suburbs were modern and urban residential spaces, some were even internationally significant, like the Munkkiniemi-Haaga Plan (1915) by architect Eliel Saarinen. World War I shattered the old world, destroyed cities and gave birth to new national states.

Helsinki remained the capital when Finland separated from Russia and became an independent republic in 1917. In the shadow of the world war and the Russian revolution in 1918 a bloody civil war divided the nation. The planning of the Parliament House in the Twenties and Thirties had great symbolic value; the building was a new institutional and democratic symbol and it was built away from the "Russian and imperial" Senate Square. Finland fought

The Suomenlinna Fortress outside Helsinki, built from 1748

two wars against the Soviet Union, in 1939–1940 and 1941–1944. Although the country was not invaded nor the capital destroyed in the 1944 bombardments, the war years were a turning point. The population had risen to over 300,000 and migration to Helsinki went on steadily. Its land area grew fivefold when some suburbs were annexed in 1946. This addition brought suburban planning into a new era, where capital, regional and metropolitan planning could be seen a whole. In the Fifties and Sixties, around 200,000 new city-dwellers were housed primarily in suburbs, the planning and construction of which irrevocably altered the old rural landscapes around the city.

With the 1952 Olympics Helsinki joined the exclusive club of Olympic cities. In the post-war period, when migration was at its peak, Helsinki's metropolitan area received its exceptionally spacious urban structure, like a "forest city". Deconstructed block structures and closeness to nature were prevalent in suburban areas. The modern dream became a reality: Helsinki's post-war urban policies were to combine democratic ideals, traffic efficiency and metropolitan image in urban planning. In 1969 the building of the metro started. In 1964 city's urban planning office was founded, with the aim to make the city "western" and modern. Today, local authorities play an exceptionally influential role in city plan – based on the city's strong land ownership, estate policy and its investments in infrastructure.

After the end of the Cold War, Helsinki became a metropolis for good. Globalization and the increasing European integration prompted changes to planning. Helsinki sought its references not in a national urban hierarchy but among other capitals around the Baltic and in Europe. Old factory and warehouse areas, ports and waterfronts become new housing areas, and the revitalization of the historic center continued. The biggest problem in the early 2000s has been the lack of avalaible land. North and south Helsinki, the Helsinki of gentlemen and that of workers; in the past 50 years the city has developed another dividing line between east and west. Helsinki is a migrants' city, a Finnish melting pot. The 1952 Olympic Games

City Planner Carl L. Engel (1816)

and the Conference for Security and Co-operation in Europe 1975 bestowed international self-esteem, the "Helsinki spirit" – a term born of the polarity of super-power politics in Europe in the late Cold War period, as European leaders met and began to consider the importance of co-operation and peace for the continent. Helsinki's creative and artistic life are concentrated in the oldest parts of the city. Here are the university, the literary societies, the publishing and media houses, the main libraries, the most important bookshops, cafés, bars and restaurants. Helsinki worships its writers and scholars; the city received its first writer's statue as early as 1885, when national poet, Johan Ludvig Runeberg, was immortalized in bronze in the Esplanade. The first street names dedicated to creative persons were adopted at that time. Today a young generation of writers, artists and scholars delights in the city and the life in its urban center.

East or west? This question remains unsolved in Helsinki. The Russian influence was at the same time culturally western, but geographically eastern. The need for planning and architecture was central after the independence, but resources were limited. But Helsinki has also been planned and built in the functionalist spirit of the west. Both styles represent an approach, expressing equality and efficiency matched to the needs of the capital city of the independent republic. Helsinki is definitely an artificial, planned city; its journey to become the emotional, intellectual and cultural capital of Finland has lasted almost 200 years. The process has involved social and cultural tensions, the search for modernism and an urban way of life. In the period of growth during the 20th century, Helsinki was seen as a "giant with feet of clay" or a "greedy exploiter" of the country side. Strong decades for modernism and literature have included the 1880s as well as the 1920s, the 1950s and 1960s. Helsinki's essence aquires its nature from its culture, its strong economic growth, its political civil activity.

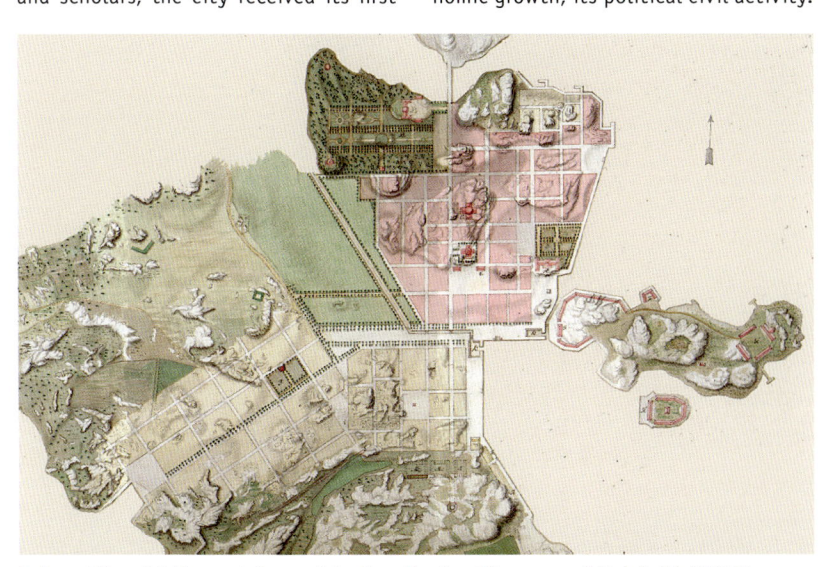

Johan Albrecht Ehrenström and Anders Kocke: City map of Helsinki (1815)

Recycling area at the polar circle

Douglas Gordon / Heikki Mäntymäki

Helsinki is a highly planned city. It is also a modern city, a garden city and a maritime city. Helsinki is a city that's developed significantly since the World War II. In the past 25 years it has doubled in volume, not in terms of expanding outwards, but in terms of the actual amount of building that has taken place. And the city is still green.

In terms of the planning hierarchy the Regional Plan is a structure plan, which is a legal statutory plan that sets out the green areas and the transport corridors. There is, therefore, a working hierarchy whereby all other plans broadly complement the Regional plan. The City Masterplan is a land-use plan. It is not a statutory plan, but a City Council approved plan which demonstrates where the key changes will take place in the city over the next 25–30 years. There are some 15 major development projects taking place under way within the city, one of the smallest being the Arabianranta area for 7,000 people. The largest is situated in Vuosaari for 40,000 residents in the east. In historical terms, these structural changes represent the greatest spatial development since the early 19th century. Helsinki promotes a plan-led system. In most cities, planning is developer-led, meaning the developer will submit the plans to a city for permission to build. Over 60% of Helsinki's land area is in public ownership. A plan-led system in Helsinki ensures that the plans are made in the City Planning Department for new development areas, so that private investment then follows-on by adopting these plans for implementation. This enables land-use planning to be integrated with land management and with traffic and transport. The City of Helsinki employs an integrated spatial planning system with land practices. Land is planned by the City and then parcelled into land plots which generally are let for 50 or 60 years.

Space potential in Helsinki

Brownfield Development

Most of Helsinki's developments are made on brownfield sites. This is an important policy statement and it adds up to an overall set of policies which aim to create a socially sustainable city and a high quality, easily accessible public transport network and equally high quality environment. The City of Helsinki invests heavily in creating a high quality public transport system. For a city of nearly 600,000 the connectivity within the city is very good. The metro, with two branch lines, covers the eastern areas. The overland rail system runs north, north-west and directly to the upper-west region. There are ten tram lines covering the entire inner city, and a feeder bus system operating around each of the metro and commuter train lines.

A significant share of the important buildings in Finland is added to the winners of architectural competitions. These competitions promote new ways of thinking and the creation of new ar-

Overlooking the historic city center of Helsinki viewed from Kalasatama

chitectural visions. This democratic and open system presents opportunities for many talents. Architectural competitions are a tool that can be used to select the best possible result: the competitions are judged specifically on the merits of architecture and planning. The aim of an effective competition system is to ensure that the best work wins. Finland has a long history of architectural competitions, which are organized by both municipalities and private interests. Just as many cities around the world, Helsinki is going through a major process of renewal as its former industrial and harbor areas are transformed for new uses. The completion of the new harbor at Vuosaari has freed up the largest amount of space in a 100 years for constructing new housing and workplaces in the very heart of the city. Over the next few decades the city will thus embark on a major task with central importance for the urban structure as new areas are planned and built. As a result, around 20 kilometers of new public waterfront will be opened up for use by all of the city's residents. This represents a significant addition to the waterfront promenades that circle the peninsula.

The most important development areas at the moment are the former downtown harbors Kalasatama, Jätkäsaari and Kruunuvuorenranta.

Kalasatama

Kalasatama will be a tight-knit, urban district. The area is situated in a central location on the eastern shoreline of the central city area. Kalasatama will be connected to the central city area and its shores will be open to the residents of the city. Initial construction work at Kalasatama began in 2009 and the first residential building began in spring 2011. Construction will proceed one area at a time with the construction work continuning until the 2030s. By then, there will be 18,000 people living and 12,000 working in Kalasatama. A six kilometers seaside promenade will cover the shorelines. The streets will be designed to provide views out to sea. It will be possible to enjoy sea views from the sauna and shared facilities on the upper floors of the residential buildings, too. Urbanity in Kalasatama refers to tightly knit buildings as well as an abundance of choice, random encounters

Kalasatama with its future high-rise skyline around the train station

and living, changing spaces. Strollers and cyclists will be provided with various routes to choose from. Space will be reserved for restaurants and small boutiques in the basements of the buildings. The largest commercial premises will be located in the heart of Kalasatama. In addition to traditional multi-story buildings, there will also be tower blocks, terraced buildings, detached city houses and floating apartments. Sites have also been reserved for student, senior and social housing. The area's constructors and planners are mainly selected through plot allocation and architectural competitions. Kalasatama is situated in a transportation intersection and connections to all destinations are good. The metro station began operations in January 2007 and several bus routes via Kalasatama are already running. The first trams will begin to operate in the area by 2020.

Jätkäsaari

Jätkäsaari is being redeveloped as a residential and workplace area with construction work continuing until 2025. It will be built as a distinctive part of Helsinki's city center with streetfront shops and sidewalk cafés. When Jätkäsaari is completed it will be home to approximately 16,000 residents. The existing passenger harbor for ships to Tallinn and St. Petersburg will remain. Office buildings will be erected in the harbor areas where residential buildings are not approved for environmental reasons. Streets, parks and other public spaces have been designed to be fully accessible to all residents and visitors; the safety of children has been the starting point for traffic solutions. The distance between Jätkäsaari to the city center is only about 1.5 kilometers. The proximity and atmosphere of the sea, the spectacular views from parks and the waterfront, the boat marina and passenger terminal, as well as the neighborhood's diversified architecture will impart a distinctive seaside flavour to Jätkäsaari. Jätkäsaari is being planned as a sustainable development. Its position in the inner city already supports these goals: the urban structure is dense and the area has an effective public transport network based around the tram and metro. In the future, energy efficient solutions will be favoured for all buildings.

Kruunuvuorenranta

The city district of Kruunuvuorenranta will be built on the southwestern part of Laajasalo Island, directly facing the city center. Large containers in the oil harbor have so far been the most dominant

Spectacular views and direct proximity to the sea in new residential Jätkäsaari

feature here. Within 15 years it will offer approximately 10,000 people a seaside residence close to nature, impressively surrounded as it is by the sea and the land. On the varied shoreline you can enjoy the views out to sea, go swimming by the beaches, or walk along the boat harbours and shore promenades. In the west you can see the inner city with its church towers; Suomenlinna lies to the south and towards the east you can gaze on the island scenery. The Kruunuvuorenranta region is still pretty unknown to city dwellers. The oil harbor is closed to the public and hikers have not found their way to the cliffs of Kruunuvuori. Only a few people know that the manor park of Stansvik is opened to the public. Kruunuvuorenranta will be a short tram or water bus ride away from the center. The area is set to become a seaside leisure center. Kruunuvuorenranta is being designed as a diverse area consisting of residential neighborhoods of apartment buildings and houses. The range of residential buildings includes different types of housing units, small blocks, terrace-houses and urban single-family homes. Owners of a few plots will have the opportunity to secure their own beaches.

Helsinki as a "Smart City-region"

The EU in its "Territorial State and Perspectives" (2011) aims to promote spatial cohesiveness through polycentric city-regions. The core city is viewed as the engine of development within a city-region. In order to be "smart", cities will need to stop sprawl, be compact and high-density. Helsinki aims to work with its neighbors to address these urban planning challenges for the future. It is only through strong city planning that Helsinki can achieve a spatially and socially cohesive city-regional structure that mitigates against climate change and maintains a Nordic Welfare city.

View over the eastern part of Espoo

E

018

054

Inner Center

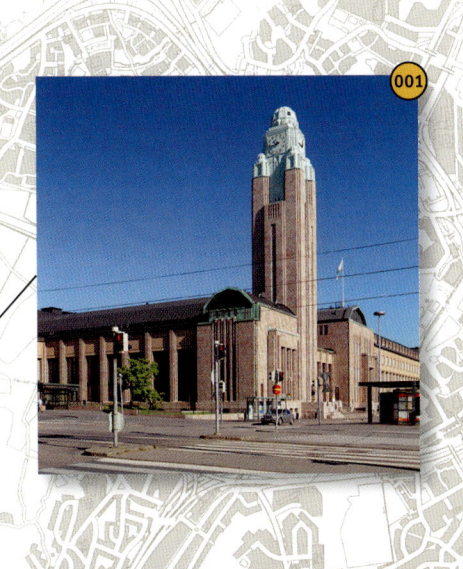

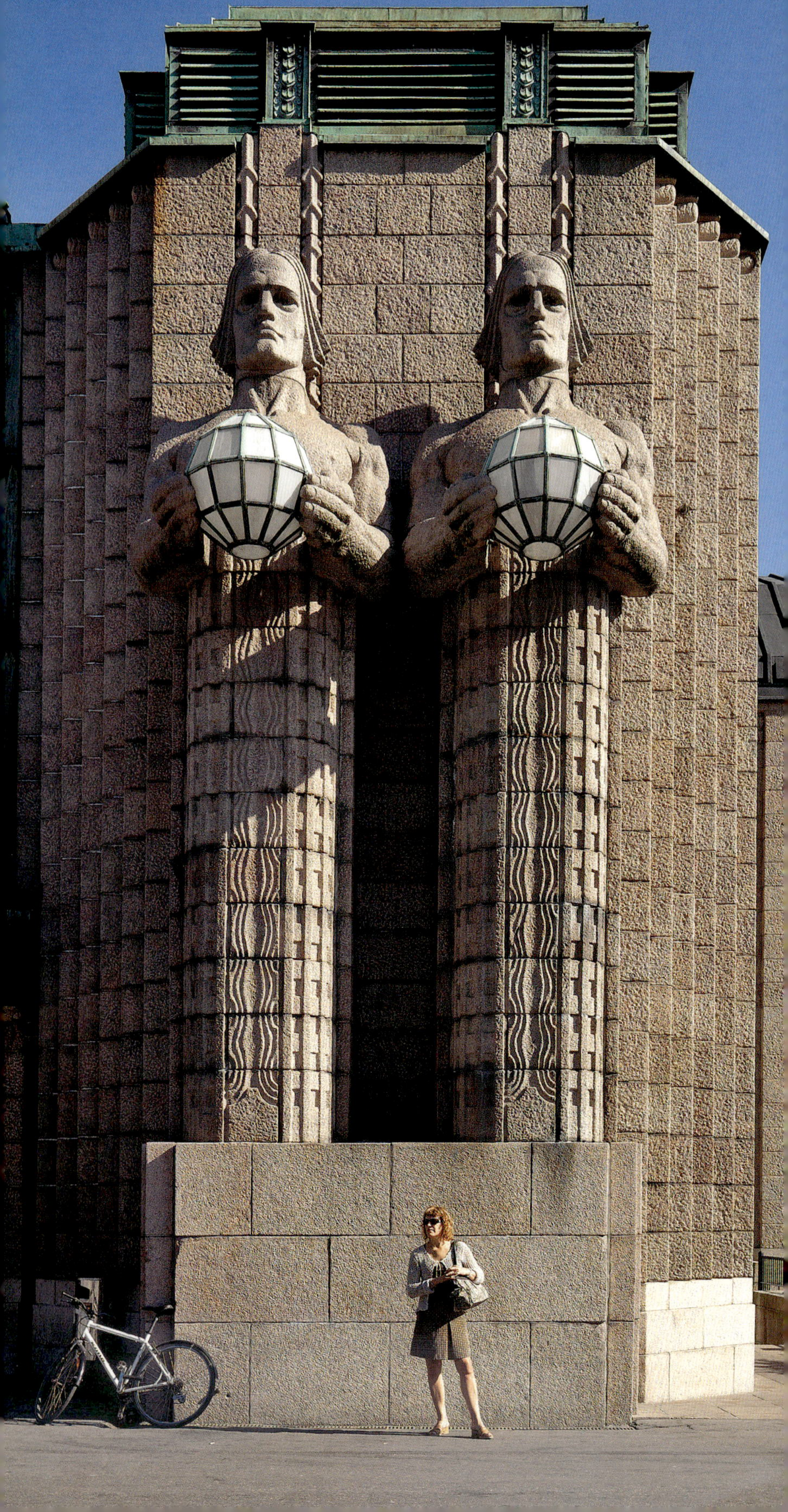

Main Railway Station
Rautatientori
Eliel Saarinen
1919

C 001

The 200,000 passengers a day make Helsinki's Central Railway Station the most visited building in all of Finland. With the inauguration of the first railway line in the country between Helsinki and Hämeenlinna in 1860 a first station was built on the current site, designed by the Swedish architect Carl Albert Edelfelt. When it became too small, in the year 1904 an architectural design competition was held for a new building. Eliel Saarinen emerged as the winner with his design in the national Romantic style. In the next five years, Saarinen revised his own design drastically in the Jugendstil, however. The railway station is now considered one of the most beautiful in Europe. The three main facades of the terminus are clad in Finnish granite. Other characteristic features are the clock tower in the east and the two figures on the left and right of the main entrance, who hold lamps in their hands in the south. The main entrance leads into a large hall with a barrel roof. At both sides of the station three-story office buildings with plaster facades flank the main hall. The train station itself has 19 platforms, but only the central intercity platforms extend right up to the hall. To the sides there are the suburban lines to Espoo and Turku. In the Sixties the *Asema-tunneli* ("tunnel") was built connecting the station with the city underneath the street in front and the tracks were electrified at the same time. In 1982 a subway station was built underneath the railway station. In 2003 the Kauppakuja shopping center and a hotel were opened just to the west side of the station. A large lounge in the station is for the President of Finland's exclusive use. Its vintage furniture was designed by Eliel Saarinen – the architect, who drafted the whole railway station in the early 20th Century. The lounge was originally planned for the Zsar of Russia.

Eliel Saarinen's design for the station had already called for a shelter for all platforms with a glass roof. However, it was only built in the year 2000 and designed by the finnish architect Esa Piironen.

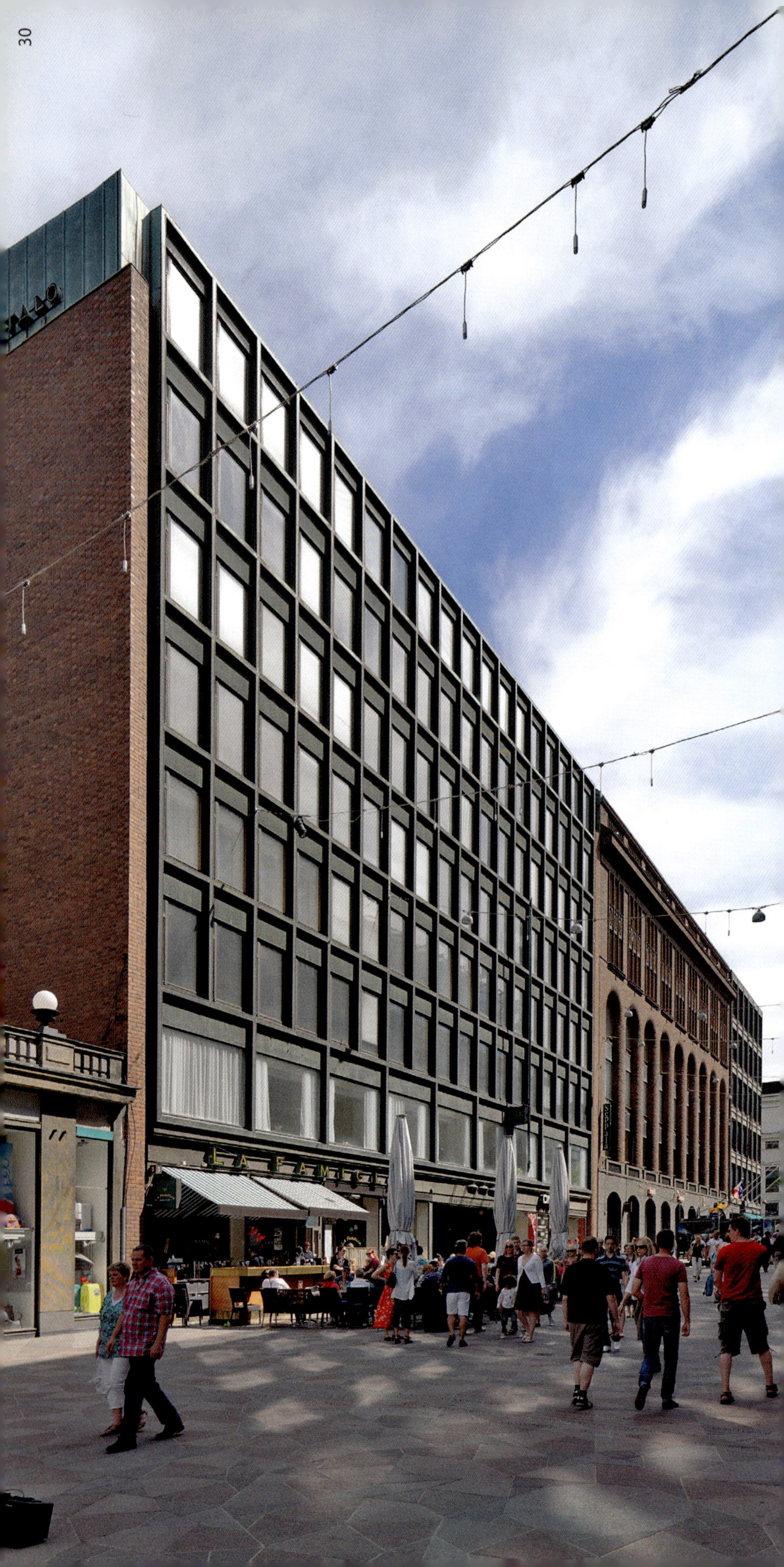

Rautatalo Office Building « C 002
Keskuskatu 3
Alvar Aalto
1955

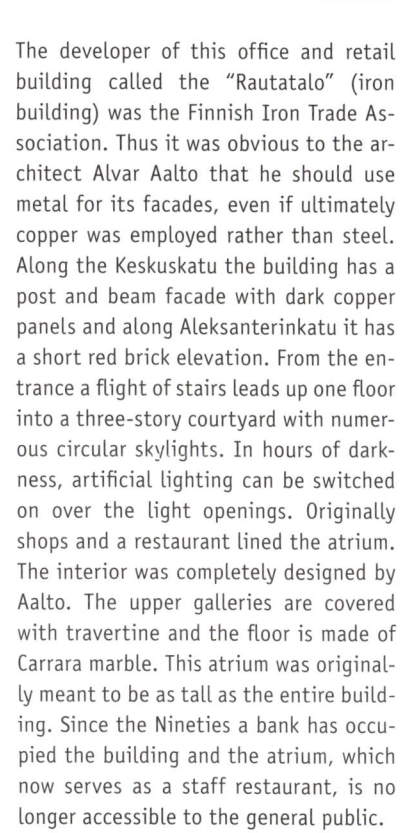

The developer of this office and retail building called the "Rautatalo" (iron building) was the Finnish Iron Trade Association. Thus it was obvious to the architect Alvar Aalto that he should use metal for its facades, even if ultimately copper was employed rather than steel. Along the Keskuskatu the building has a post and beam facade with dark copper panels and along Aleksanterinkatu it has a short red brick elevation. From the entrance a flight of stairs leads up one floor into a three-story courtyard with numerous circular skylights. In hours of darkness, artificial lighting can be switched on over the light openings. Originally shops and a restaurant lined the atrium. The interior was completely designed by Aalto. The upper galleries are covered with travertine and the floor is made of Carrara marble. This atrium was originally meant to be as tall as the entire building. Since the Nineties a bank has occupied the building and the atrium, which now serves as a staff restaurant, is no longer accessible to the general public.

Academic Bookstore D 003
Pohjoisesplanadi 39
Elissa and Alvar Aalto
1969

The winning design from Alvar Aalto and his wife Elissa for the Akateeminen Kirjakauppa, the most famous book store in Helsinki, was choosen in 1962 in a two-phase architectural design competition. In 1969 the Academic Bookstore opened. For its construction the adjacent "Kinopalatsi" cinema hall had to be demolished. The bookstore's large rectangular atrium receives daylight through three skylights with interesting, prismatic shapes that protrude down into the hall, their crystalline forms contrasting with the simple rectangular shapes of the overall plan. The two upper galleries are covered with white marble. The bookshop extends over three floors, its white surfaces providing the perfect backdrop for the colorful books and customers. The Café Aalto offers pleasant views from a balcony into the atrium. The bookstore was established in 1986 and contains some of the furniture removed from the nearby Rautatalo Building. The two discrete dark copper facades at the corner lot give no inkling of the bright inner atrium inside. They have mesh walls with large windows and narrow copper strips. Above the bookstore there are office floors. The Academic Bookstore is connected underground with the adjacent Stockman department store to which it belong.

Kinopalatsi Building ⌃
Keskuskatu 1b
Eliel Saarinen
1921

D 004

Porthania Building ⌄
Yliopistonkatu 3
Aarne Ervi
1957

C 005

The "Movie Palace" Commercial Building was the last building designed in his native Finland by Finlands most famous pre-modern architect Eliel Saarinen before he emigrate to the U.S. The "Kinopalatsi" has a granite facade on the ground floor and a red brick facade above. Vertical high and deep window niches on three floors make the spaces between them appear as giant columns. Contrary to its name, the building is now a bank. The actual "movie palace" was located on the property next door. Originally, those buildings were to be extended by Saarinen, but instead the Academic Bookstore was built by Alvar Aalto.

This building is a pioneering structure with prefabricated components. During its construction in 1957 it was Finland's most modern concrete building. The building is accessed via a courtyard at the Hallituskatu, which is also where the cafeteria is located in a low pavilion. The auditoria are situated on the ground floor with offices, a library and seminar rooms above; the studios are on the top floor. The building, named after the humanist Professor Henrik Gabriel Porthan, today serves as the Faculty of Law of the University of Helsinki. The heart of the building is the large central hall with a mural by Arvid Broms and Olli Miettinen.

Sähkötalo Energy Company ⌃   B 006
Kampinkuja 2
Alvar Aalto
1965–76

The headquarters building of the local electric company, called "Sähkötalo", incorporates the company's former building designed by Gunnar Taucher in 1939. The receding top floors combine old and new with layers of expressive white eaves. In the center of the new building there is a large atrium with a skylight, washed in natural daylight. Above this public level are the office floors and the cafeteria in the executive suite. The basement houses electrical plant for power distribution in a bomb-proof bunker. An arcade leads to the main entrance. The architect Alvar Aalto designed the blue and white ceramic tiles in the foyer and lift lobbies. The main hall, covered with limestone from Oland, is now a café. The "Sähkötalo" was extensively renovated in 2007 and connected underground to the adjacent Kamppi Shopping Center.

Makkaratalo Office Building ⌃ C 007
Kaivokatu 6
Viljo Revell, Heikki Castrén
1967

Former Nordic Union Bank » C 008
Fabianinkatu 29
Alvar Aalto
1965

The Makkaratalo Office Building across from the Central Railway Station is the most hated piece of architecture in Finland. The building's name "Makkaratalo" (sausage building) is an allusion to the semi-circular floor ends of the parking level. The design was part of the car-friendly architecture proposed "City Center Plan" of 1958 which called for the demolition of many valuable old buildings in the area. It is therefore ironic that the giant "sausage building" is now listed. Even after Viljo Revell's death in 1964 the plan was pursued further. The office and retail building in the bland International style was purchased in 2000 by a real estate company that is currently renovating it. The large car ramps that lead up to the parking deck will be torn down. In 2004 a survey of readers of the *Helsingin Sanomat* newspaper the Makkaratalo Office Building was voted "ugliest building in town".

The building is located next to the old headquarters of the bank. In 1960, Alvar Aalto was asked to design a new building for the site near the North Esplanade. Aalto's design jumps from three to eight stories in order to adjust to the heights of adjacent buildings while his facade design differs significantly from two neighboring buildings. The sober, square grid facade incorporates narrow strips of copper, its rhythm similar to that of the nearby building Stora Enso Gutzeit Building. The receding ground floor houses an arcade and the fire wall between the higher and the lower component has a red granite cover. The bank occupies the ground floor, while the six upper floors accommodate offices and the penthouse contains two auditoriums and a terrace. The interiors were heavily renovated. The bank subsequently sold the building and it was divided up to serve as a speculative office building.

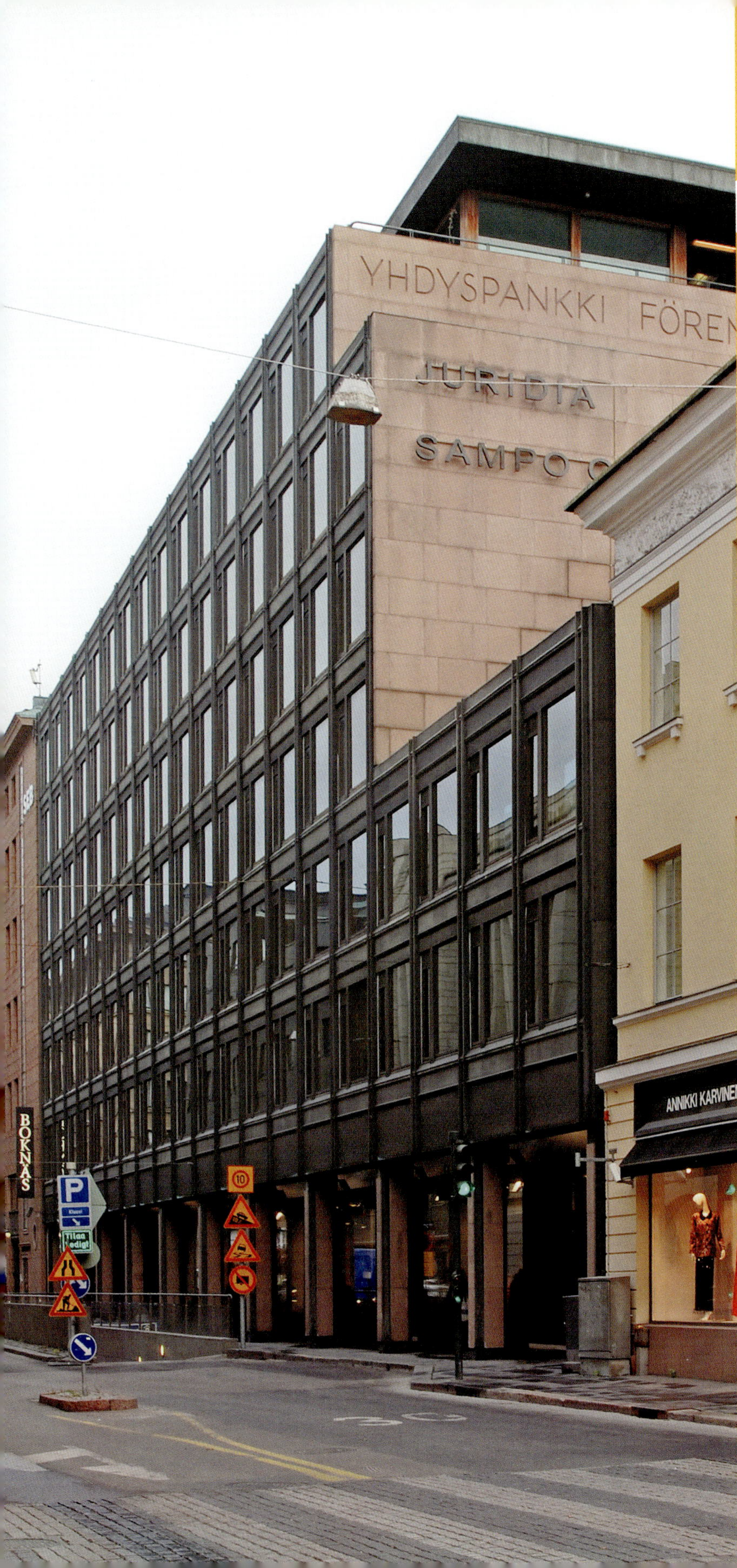
YHDYSPANKKI FÖREN
JURIDIA
SAMPO
BOKNÄS
ANNIKKI KARVINEN

Tennis Palace ⌃
Salomonkatu 15
Helge Lundström
1937

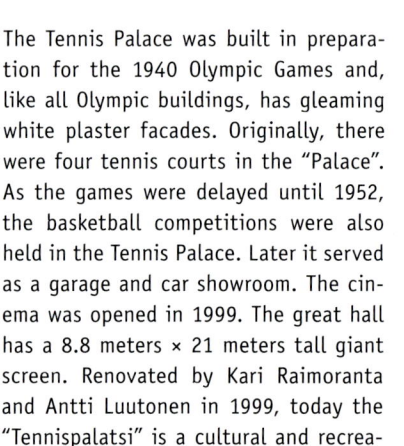

A 009

Grand Marina Hotel ⌄ »
Kanavakatu 6
Lars Sonck et al.
1928

D 010

The Tennis Palace was built in preparation for the 1940 Olympic Games and, like all Olympic buildings, has gleaming white plaster facades. Originally, there were four tennis courts in the "Palace". As the games were delayed until 1952, the basketball competitions were also held in the Tennis Palace. Later it served as a garage and car showroom. The cinema was opened in 1999. The great hall has a 8.8 meters × 21 meters tall giant screen. Renovated by Kari Raimoranta and Antti Luutonen in 1999, today the "Tennispalatsi" is a cultural and recreational center that houses a large cinema complex, an art museum, the "Museum of Cultures" and a few shops under its distinctive low barrel roof.

The large warehouse in the Katajanokka-District of the port was built directly on the quay. Because of its projected size and proximity to the precious neo-classical city center, in 1911 an architectural design competition was held to find a suitable solution. Lars Sonck, pioneer of the National Romantic style in Finland, emerged as the winner. Sonck's robust design combined Art Nouveau with classic accents. The 140 meters long, five-story warehouse is his largest executed building. The symmetrical facade is made of dark brick with bright Swedish soffits. The ground floor has arched windows with a perforated facade above. The cornerstone of the "K12" warehouse was laid in 1912, but construction had to wait because of World War I. At its completion the colossus was the largest concrete building in the Nordic countries. It originally contained halls for cold storage as well as some offices. In the Sixties demand for warehouses decreased and the building stood empty. In 1986 it was purchased and turned into the Grand Marina Hotel by Gullichsen, Vormala and Kairamo. Where once coffee and rubber were stored, 462 hotel rooms have been installed. The surfaces of the warehouse remain largely unchanged but the 1,800 windows were replaced. Today, there are 16 different room types with luxury suites on the top floor. The floorplan of the warehouse proved to be quite flexible and durable.

Marina Congress Center ≽
Katajanokanlaituri 6
Gullichsen, Kairamo & Vormala
1964

D 011

The Marina Congress Center was established in the former "K7" warehouse in 1964 next to the Grand Marina Hotel. The red brick building was gutted and partially given a new facade made of glass and glass blocks on the street side and gray granite on the port side. The three-story convention center can accommodate 1,500 people and also offers 1,800 square meters of office space. The two large halls are further, smaller meeting rooms. In 1992 the fourth OSCE conference series was held here.

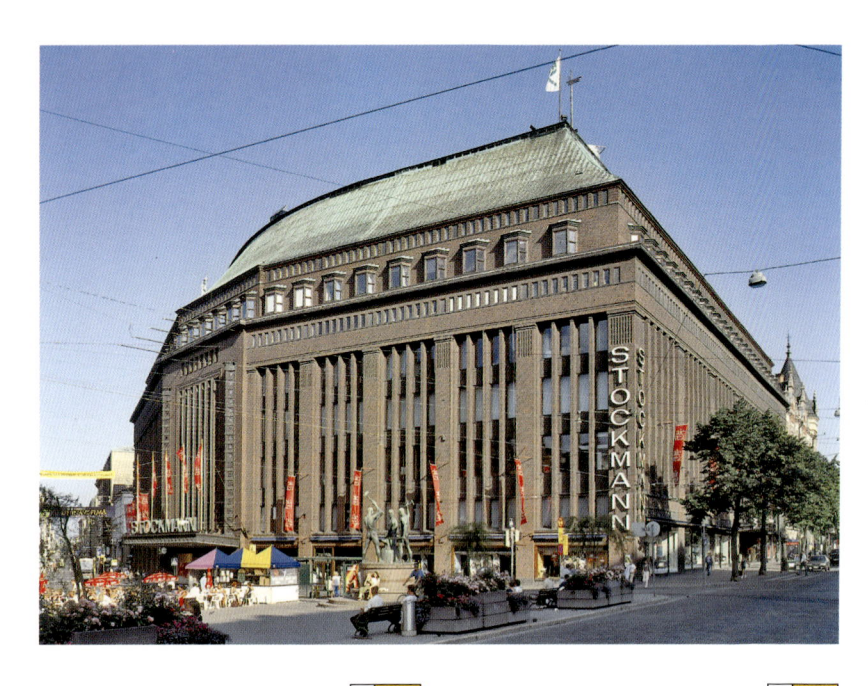

Department Store *Stockmann*   C 012
Aleksanterinkatu 52b
Sigurd Frosterus
1930

Extension of *Stockmann* »   C 013
Centralgatan
Gullichsen, Kairamo & Vormala
1989

More than 17 million customers per annum make Stockmann's the largest department store in Northern Europe. In the Twenties only the lower four floors were built after a design by Sigurd Frosterus that had won in an architectural design competition. In the Thirties four more floors were added with a large courtyard in the middle that has the same shape as the building block. The dark red brick facades have a vertical emphasis. The food hall in the basement and the famous clock at the main entrance quickly became popular meeting points in the city. The store was continually extended and now occupies the entire city block. In 1989, the adjacent Argos House was completely gutted and incorporated into the department store. In 2007 a second expansion began, which will enlarge the retail area by another 10,000 square meters to over 50,000 square meters. The atrium will partly covered for this purpose (from the sixth to the eighth floor). At the top a food court will be added. The latest expansion, designed by Pekka Laatio, will see the vertical circulation with its 40 elevators and escalators unified.

In 1989 an extension to the Stockmann Department Store was added on a narrow, but prominent urban corner lot to the southeast of the store. The design is a typical child of the Eighties. Situated next to the 1987 Argos Building its stainless steel and glass brick tower draws customers from the North Esplanade into the department store. The new building sets itself apart from the existing ones, its tower and the set-back corner making it a distinctive landmark.

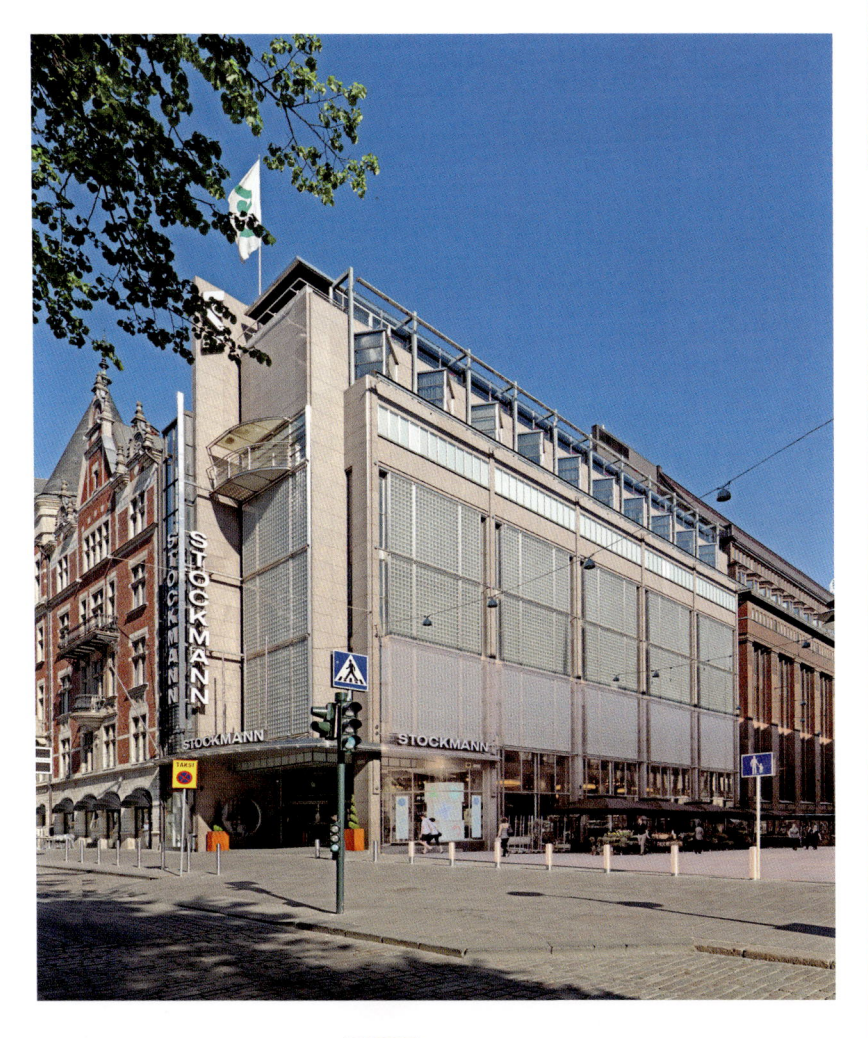

Restaurant *Savoy* ⌐
Eteläesplanadi 14
Alvar Aalto
1937

D 014

The Savoy restaurant is famous for its Alvar and Aino Aalto designed interiors that make it a unique *Gesamtkunstwerk* of early modern Finnish design. It was Alvar Aalto's first commission in Helsinki. In addition to the ceiling and wall covers with birch veneer, the furniture and lamps as well as cutlery, table-ware and glasses, and of course the famous "Savoy Vase" were all designed by the Aaltos. In 1936 the A. Ahlströhm company constructed the building, in which the Savoy is housed, designed by Valter Jung at the corner of the Southern Esplanade and Kasarmikatu. Ahlström asked Alvar Aalto to design the restaurant with 100 seats and lounges on the seventh and eighth floor. Despite the wide view over the city, the restaurant's atmosphere is intimate and cozy. Among the technologically modern elements of the design are the four express elevators that bring customers upstairs and a modern air filter. The clean lines have made the restaurant one of the most popular and best restaurants in the city for decades. Its most famous guest, national hero Marshal Mannerheim, still has a table preserved in his memory.

World Trade Center
Aleksanterinkatu 17
Pauli E. Blomstedt
1929

C 015

The former office building of the Finnish Central Bank ("Liittopankki") is now known as Helsinki's World Trade Center. The precise geometrically arranged, vertically emphasized facade rests on a solid base, which is taken up with large arches and shop windows. Pauli E. Blomstedt's design already shows signs an emerging Modernism reminiscent of the commercial buildings by Louis Sullivan in Chicago. The "Liittopankki" building is seen as a symbol of early modern urban architecture in Helsinki and is similarly ambitious as the early skyscrapers in the United States. The former banking hall, illuminated by a light ceiling, is situated on the street corner. In 1995 the building was rebuilt to a design by Jan Söderlund and Rolf Krogius. Since this transformation the former office building houses more than 130 international companies and so it is justifiably called today the "World Trade Center". The hotel, which was formerly on the upper floors, has also been converted into offices. One of the courtyards has been fitted with a glass roof.

Administration Building « B 016
Malminrinne 6
Gunnar Taucher
1938

Main Post Office ⌄ A 017
Mannerheimintie 11
Jorma Järvi, Erik Lindroos
1938

Starting in 1913 Gunnar Taucher worked as an architect for the City of Helsinki and was named the official city architect ten years later. In this role, he designed the Electricity Board Building on Kampintori, which speaks a clear and timeless architectural language. When Aalto built the extension building next door he swallowed up Taucher's building to create the "Sähkötalo" in 1976 and added the expressive attic floors.

The Main Post Office at the Central Station is a good example of the calm modernist architecture of the late Thirties in Finland. The building's massive structure with its uniform punched facades creates a tranquil urban anchor in this busy district of Helsinki. The facade of the building is made of yellow bricks. Erik Lindroos and Jävvi Jorma won with their design in an architectural design competition held in 1934.

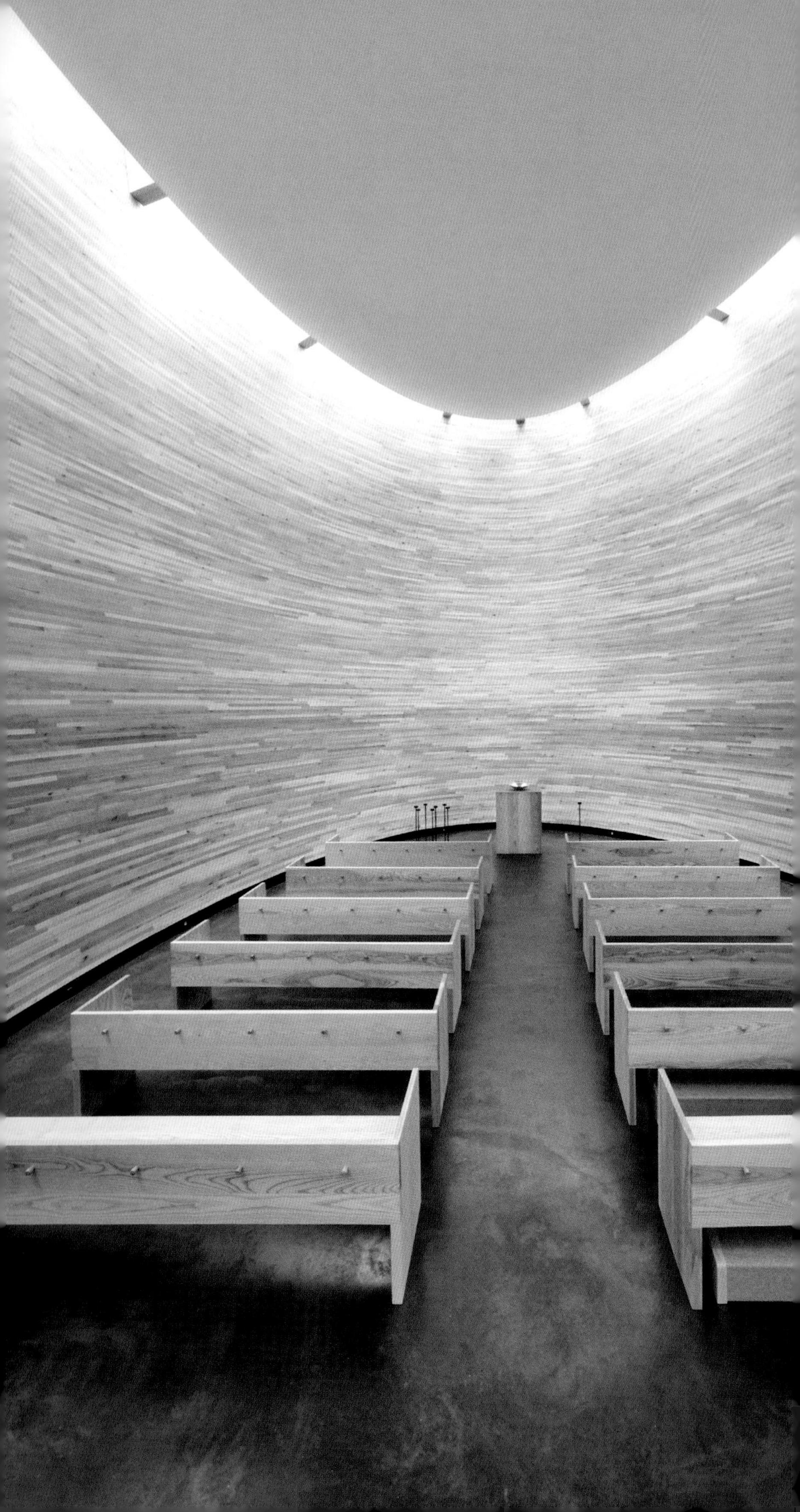

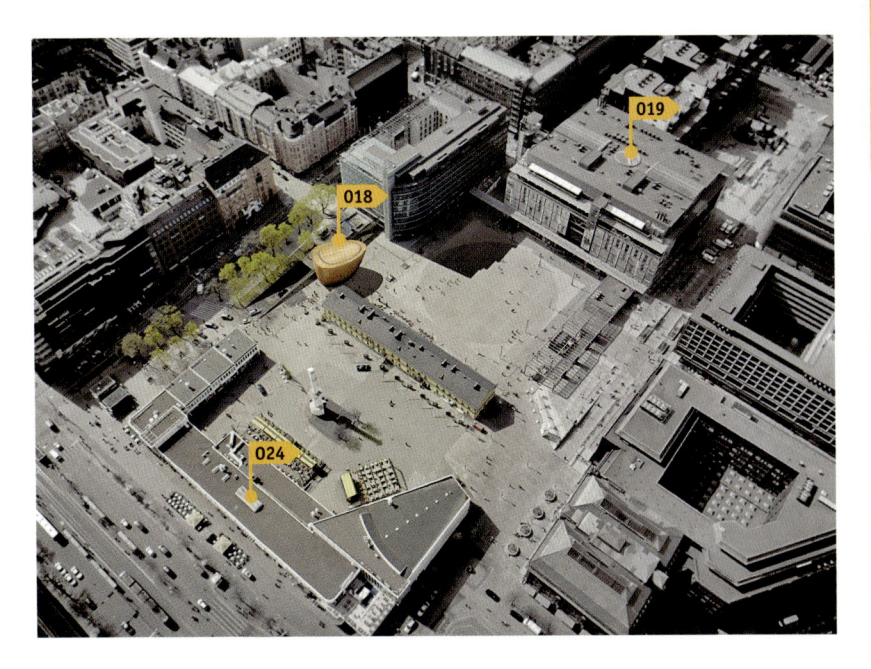

Chapel of Silence
Narinkka Square
K2S Architects
2012

A 018

Kamppi Shopping Center ≽
Urho Kekkosen katu 5b
Juhani Pallasmaa
2005

A 019

The new Chapel of Silence at the southern corner of the busy Narinkka Square in Kamppi creates a quiet place for contemplation. The curved wooden facade looks as if it had been sanded by the pedestrian flow on the plaza. The protective, oval interior acts like a sanctuary in the heart of the city and receives natural light from above through a large skylight. From Simonkatu visitors first reach a small square, from which a staircase leads down to the entrance. The interior walls are made of thick, oiled alder planks and all the furniture is made of solid wood.

The six-story Kamppi Shopping Center is the largest new business district in Helsinki and also the largest single construction project in the history of Finland. The retail area connects with a bus and subway station and all deliveries take place discretely underground. The facades are evidence of Juhani Pallasmaa's interest in constructivist and structuralist architecture and machine aesthetic. A central atrium, which extends over the entire height of the building, brings natural daylight into the depth of the building and facilitates the orientation of the shoppers and passers-by.

Department Store *Sokos* ↖ A 020
Mannerheimintie 9
Erkki Huttunen
1952

This building forms an important link between the central train station on one side and the Mannerheimintie on the other. Towards the Mannerheimintie it has two rounded corners and towards the station it has a straight facade. Above the glass facades on the two lower floors, granite facades clad the upper office and hotel floors. The top three floors are set back and form roof terraces. The building was renovated by Juhani Pallasma in 1996, when he created an indoor, six-story atrium at its heart.

Faculty of Wood and Forestry ↗ C 021
Unioninkatu 40
Jussi Paatela
1939

The "Metsätalo" is the Faculty of Wood and Forestry of the University of Helsinki and the size of the building is an illustration of the important role that wood and forestry play in Finland. It consists of three U-shaped five-story wings with a pergola along the Unionkatu forming a courtyard. There are perforated facades and a large auditorium on the first floor. The furniture and all interior design elements are made of wood. There used to be a greenhouse and cafeteria on the roof.

Hotel *Palace* ⌄
Eteläranta 10
Viljo Revell, Keijo Petäjä
1952

D 022

Known as the "Teollisuuskeskus" (industrial center), this Commercial Building at the downtown port was inaugurated in 1952, when Helsinki hosted the Summer Olympic Games. An expression of modern potent Finnish industry, it was commissioned by the Association of Finnish Industries and covers an entire block. The building includes offices, shops and a large hotel. Erected on an H-shaped floor plan, the building is reminiscent of the big ferries in the nearby harbor. The elevators and staircase towers connect the two bars of the "H". The "Palace" takes up an entire city block, while the two lower floors are set back from the harbor, creating an arcade. The six office floors above have strict band facades. The hotel, located on in the ninth and tenth floor, is set back from the building line. The facades are made of exposed concrete.

Meripaja Office Building `D 023`
Kanavakatu 4
Olli-Pekka Jokela, Kai Wartiainen
1993

Lasipalatsi ("Glass Palace") » `A 024`
Mannerheimintie 22
Niilo Kokko et al.
1935

This 7,500 square meters, four-story, white office building, in which more than 200 people work, is the seat of the development agency of the Foreign Ministry of Finland. The design by Olli-Pekka Jokela and Kai Wartiainen won in an architectural design competition. The building incorporates the former Mint of Finland (designed in 1864 by Ernst B. Lohrmann), which today is used as an educational center. A grand staircase leads to the main entrance of the new wing. The white walls match the neighboring buildings, which form a white front towards the port and sea. The building consists of two long bars with a glass-roofed, rectangular atrium between them. Hallways with glazed walls enclose this internal "street". The old building of the Mint is now a library specializing in topics relating to help for the Third World.

The Lasipalatsi ("Glass Palace") on Mannerheimintie is considered one of the most beautiful functionalist buildings in the city of Helsinki. It contains offices, restaurants and a huge cinema. Originally planned as a temporary structure, it was built for the 1940 Olympic Games and rebuilt in the Fifties. The site was formerly the location of the Russian Turku barracks erected in 1830 and destroyed during the Civil War in 1918. In 1933 three architecture students, Niilo Kokko, Viljo Revell and Heimo Riihimäki, established the "Lasipatsi Initiative" and designed a concept for the building, which they proposed to the City Council. The emergence of long-distance bus traffic had made a new bus station necessary and the city suggested that it should also be built on the site. A city employee had already created a design, but the counter proposal by the young architects Niilo Kokko, Viljo Revell and Heimo Riihimäki won – much to the surprise of the established local architectural community. The lighthearted design was a breakthrough for the architects, although of the three only Viljo Revell went on to enjoy a meteoric career. The streamlined upper floor of the Lasipalatsi stands on slender reinforced concrete pillars. The design follows the dogma of "light, air and sun" so large windows on both sides turn the shops, which are accessible from both fronts, into true showcases. The modern skeleton structure allowed for open floor plans and only the colorful awnings animate its white plaster surfaces. The ambience in the restaurant, which extends the entire length of the Glass Palace. At one end its terrace overlooks the most important buildings in the city. Even the specially designed cutlery and china match the tasteful interiors, textiles and lighting while from their tables people can watch the action on the Mannerheimintie. A café on the ground floor is situated next to the entrance hall and the main stairase is decorated with a huge mural. In the Eighties the building became run down and there were plans to demolish the Glass Palace to make room for something larger. But luckily, in 1991, the U-shaped, two-story building with its arcade on one side, which stands on one of the most valuable pieces of land in Finland, was listed as a historic monument. New life came to the building in 1998, when it was converted into a media center. It presents Finland as a communications hub. The Glass Palace is now a mix of businesses: book, computer, telecom and photography shops, a library, a video store, restaurants, media companies, a diamond-shaped cinema. The offices of the Helsinki Festival and one of the best restaurants in the city, a gallery and an internet café are also to be found in the building. The private and state television companies operate TV studios inside. Passers-by can watch the action in the studios through large display windows. The Glass Palace has been carefully restored by Pia Ilonen and Minna Lukander. The signs, lamps, monochrome walls, curved glass windows and old neon signs were all restored.

Passenger Terminal ⌃　　D 025
Katajanokanlaituri 8
Gunnar Taucher
1938

The four-story passenger terminal serves the daily ferries to Sweden and Estonia, as well as international cruise ships in the summer months. The curving red brick building was originally designed as a customs building. In addition to storage facilities it also contained offices and a cafeteria. The structure is made of mushroom columns of reinforced concrete with a facade dominated by deep band windows. In 1977 the building was converted into a passenger terminal after a design by Kari Unelius. He added passenger bridges to the second floor, along which passengers can proceed directly to their ships.

Bensow Building ⌄　　D 026
Eteläesplanadi 22
Uno Ullberg
1940

The Bensow office building dissolves the closed street facade of the South Esplanade into several elements. On a narrow plot Uno Ullberg created a building with eight stories towards the boulevard, but only four towards the courtyard. The soapstone facade opens onto the boulevard as an arcade. A small plaza extens into the building to form a courtyard and a shopping arcade with a fountain decorated with a sculpture of a mermaid by Viktor Jansson. A circular glass brick dome brings daylight into the depth of the building. The 9,000 square meters space currently let to a large law firm and an advertising agency.

Olympia Terminal ⌃
Olympiaranta 1
Aarne Hytönen et al.
1952

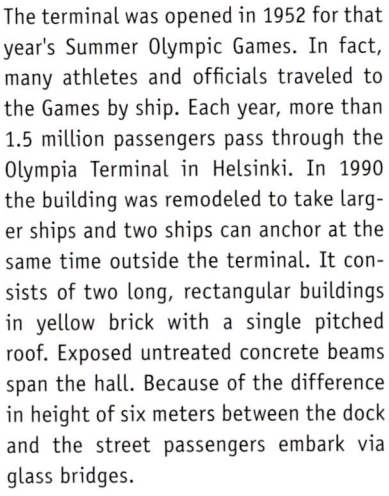

D 027

Lassila & Tikanoja Building ⌄
Eteläesplanadi 18
Johan Sigfrid Sirén
1935

D 028

The terminal was opened in 1952 for that year's Summer Olympic Games. In fact, many athletes and officials traveled to the Games by ship. Each year, more than 1.5 million passengers pass through the Olympia Terminal in Helsinki. In 1990 the building was remodeled to take larger ships and two ships can anchor at the same time outside the terminal. It consists of two long, rectangular buildings in yellow brick with a single pitched roof. Exposed untreated concrete beams span the hall. Because of the difference in height of six meters between the dock and the street passengers embark via glass bridges.

The client of this building, a textile merchant, organized an architecture competition among four architects in 1934 for his new commercial building on the Southern Esplanade in downtown Helsinki. Johan Sigfrid Sirén produced the winning design, which heralded the first truly modern office building in town. The seven-story reinforced concrete frame construction allowed flexible floor plans. The characteristic black granite facade on the ground floor has large windows with gray plaster facades of the floors above. The company Lassila & Tikanoja still exists, but today it specializes in environmental engineering.

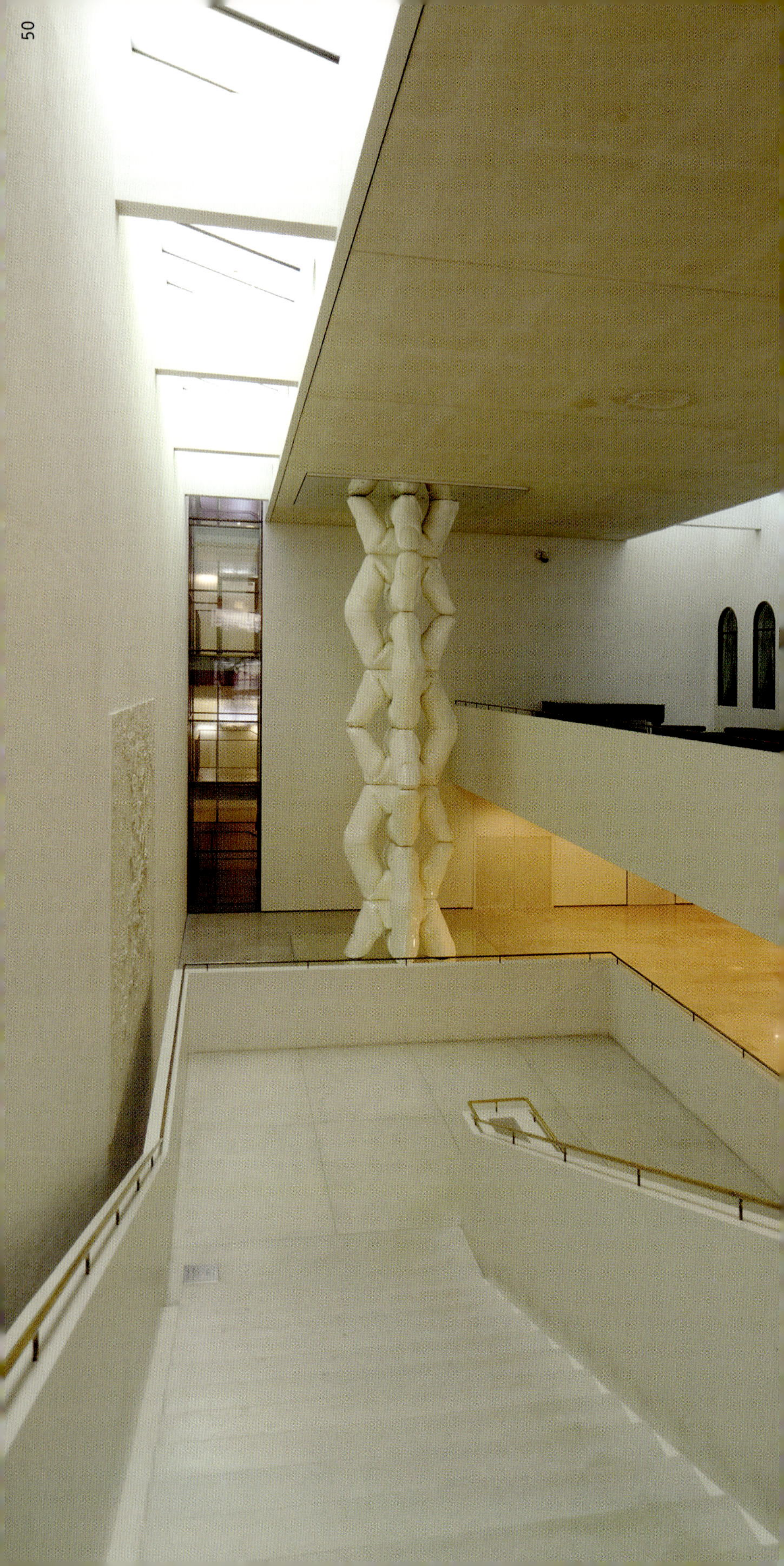

City Hall (Refurbishment)   C 029
Pohjoisesplanadi 11–13
Aarno Ruusuvuori
1970

Embassy of Sweden ≫   C 030
Pohjoisesplanadi 9
Torben Grut
1924

The City Hall of Helsinki is located between the Market and the Senate Square. It was originally built in 1833 as the hotel "Seurahuone", designed by German architect Carl Ludwig Engel. When Helsinki became the capital of Finland in 1812 a large banquet hall was built upstairs. The hotel was the spot where the first opera was performed in Finland (in 1852) and the first movie was shown (in 1896). In 1913 the hotel closed and the building was purchased by the city, then in the Twenties it was extensively rebuilt. The City Hall was again redesigned, by Aarno Ruusuvuori in 1965–70. Only the banquet hall and the facades retain their historic character. The architect who designed a new building inside the old shell, also designed the new Council building in the interior of the block in 1988 where the City Council meets.

The Embassy of Sweden enjoys a privileged site: it is located on the North Esplanade, right next to the Presidential Palace, the port and City Hall, a position expressive of the great importance Sweden played and continues to play in the life of Finland. The three-story building was built in 1839 for businessman Johan Henrik Heidenstrauch. In 1921 the noble residence was bought by the Kingdom of Sweden and converted into the Royal Swedish Embassy. The original design by Anders Fredrik Granstedt was fundamentally changed in the course of comprehensive restructuring. Swedish architect Torben Grut gave the building a yellow plaster facade, which makes the Embassy look like a mini-version of the Royal Palace in Stockholm, a Renaissance-style architecture that Nicodemus Tessin had re-formulated in a Baroque style.

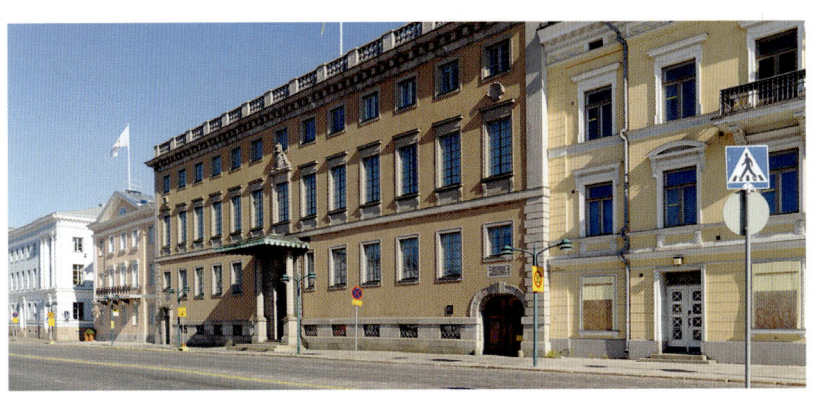

Ministry of Defense ⌃   D 031
Kasarmikatu 24
Viljo Revell, Jalmari Castrén
1965

Ministry of Foreign Affairs ⌄   D 032
Laivastokatu 22
Erik Krakström
1989

The German architect Carl Ludwig Engel had designed the "Kaarti" barracks between the years 1819 and 1825. During the World War II they were badly damaged and the main building at Kasarmitori Square was restored in 1956. The accompanying office building stands perpendicular to the main building along the Fabiankatu. The both architects Viljo Revell and Jalmari Castrén used the same height and pale yellow exterior color in their new building which today serves the Ministry of Defense of Finland. Above the first floor which has to fulfill the security demands of the user and looks ugly and largely sealed off, there are office floors above.

The Marine barracks dating from 1770, also designed by Carl Ludwig Engel extend more than 200 meters. On both sides of the narrow bar, the buildings are connected by a wall to two temple-like buildings that are reminiscent of the Admiralty in St. Petersburg. The east wing, however, was only built in 1987. Opposite the barracks stands the naval hospital designed by Anders F. Granstedt in 1938, which dates from 1838. The buildings are now used by "Merikasarmi", the Finnish Foreign Ministry. To close the court on the two open sides Erik Krakström designed two long office buildings, whose shape and pale yellow color are similar to those of the two historic buildings.

Former Institute of Anatomy | C 033
Siltavuorenpenger 3a
Toivo and Jussi Paatela
1928

Minerva ≈ | C 034
Siltavuorenpenger 5a
Jyri Haukkavaara / A6 Architects
2005

The three-story building in Kruununhaka is slightly elevated on the Siltavuori hill on the campus of the University. The building encloses a rectangular courtyard. Towards the street it shows a semi-circular "apse" with arched windows, containing the anatomy theater, in which students can watch autopsies. Until 2001 the building was used for this purpose, but in 2010 it was rebuilt for the Institute for Behavioral Research.

The new building of the Department of Behavioral Sciences of the University, called "Minerva", stands on a hillside with a view towards the northwest, the "Helsinki beach" and the Kallio district. It contains seminar rooms, a library and cafeteria. The building stands inside the block and its main access is through a courtyard on the Siltavuori campus. It consists of two parts: a two-story base was blasted into the rock and the four-story office building connects to the adjacent existing structures. Towards the courtyard, the building has a four-story, red brick facade and on the rear slope a six-story glass curtain wall.

Elonvara Building ≈ ≈ C 035
Kaisaniemenkatu 13
Yrjö Lindegren
1930

Pohja Life Insurance Building C 036
Kaisaniemenkatu 6
Oiva Kallio
1930

Coinciding with the architectural competition for the construction of Pohja Insurance Building on the other side of Kaisaniemenkatu, a competition for the new Elonvara Building was held. Organised around a courtyard, the headquarters of the Elonvara Insurance Company is the more conservative and its vertically emphasized facades are in the tradition of the German Hanseatic warehouse buildings. Daylight falls on the main staircase and the offices. The two lower floors offer retail spaces along the street. A few years after this project, Yrjö Lindegren became famous with his modernistic design of the Olympic Stadium.

Compared to the Elonvara Insurance Builing constructed at the same time, the Pohja Life Insurance-Building follows the principles of classical Modernism: strip windows, large shop windows at ground floor and usable roof terraces were typical elements of the emerging functionalism in Finland. Originally there were shops on the bottom two floors, five office floors above and leisure facilities on the set-back eighth floor. The entrance leads to a circular, two-story atrium on the first floor, which receives natural daylight from above through a skylight. A bay window accentuates the long street facade.

Engineers' Association ≈   D 037
Ratakatu 9
Alvar Aalto
1952

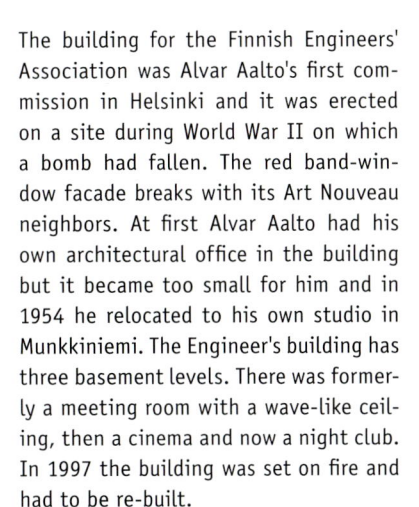

KEVA Pension Fund   C 038
Unioninkatu 39
Käpy and Simo Paavilainen
2005

The building for the Finnish Engineers' Association was Alvar Aalto's first commission in Helsinki and it was erected on a site during World War II on which a bomb had fallen. The red band-window facade breaks with its Art Nouveau neighbors. At first Alvar Aalto had his own architectural office in the building but it became too small for him and in 1954 he relocated to his own studio in Munkkiniemi. The Engineer's building has three basement levels. There was formerly a meeting room with a wave-like ceiling, then a cinema and now a night club. In 1997 the building was set on fire and had to be re-built.

The office building for the local pension fund follows the orientation of its two neighboring urban areas: the main facade along Unioninkatu is divided off-center by a large incision, which relates to the direction of the nearby Kaisaniemenkatu, while the main facade follows the street. In this tall cut a large canopy projects above the main entrance from where a passage leads to the inner courtyard. The canteen, the conference area and the 21,000 square meters office space are oriented towards this center. Bridges connect both parts of the inner canyon. The interior walls are clad in copper and the street facades in travertine.

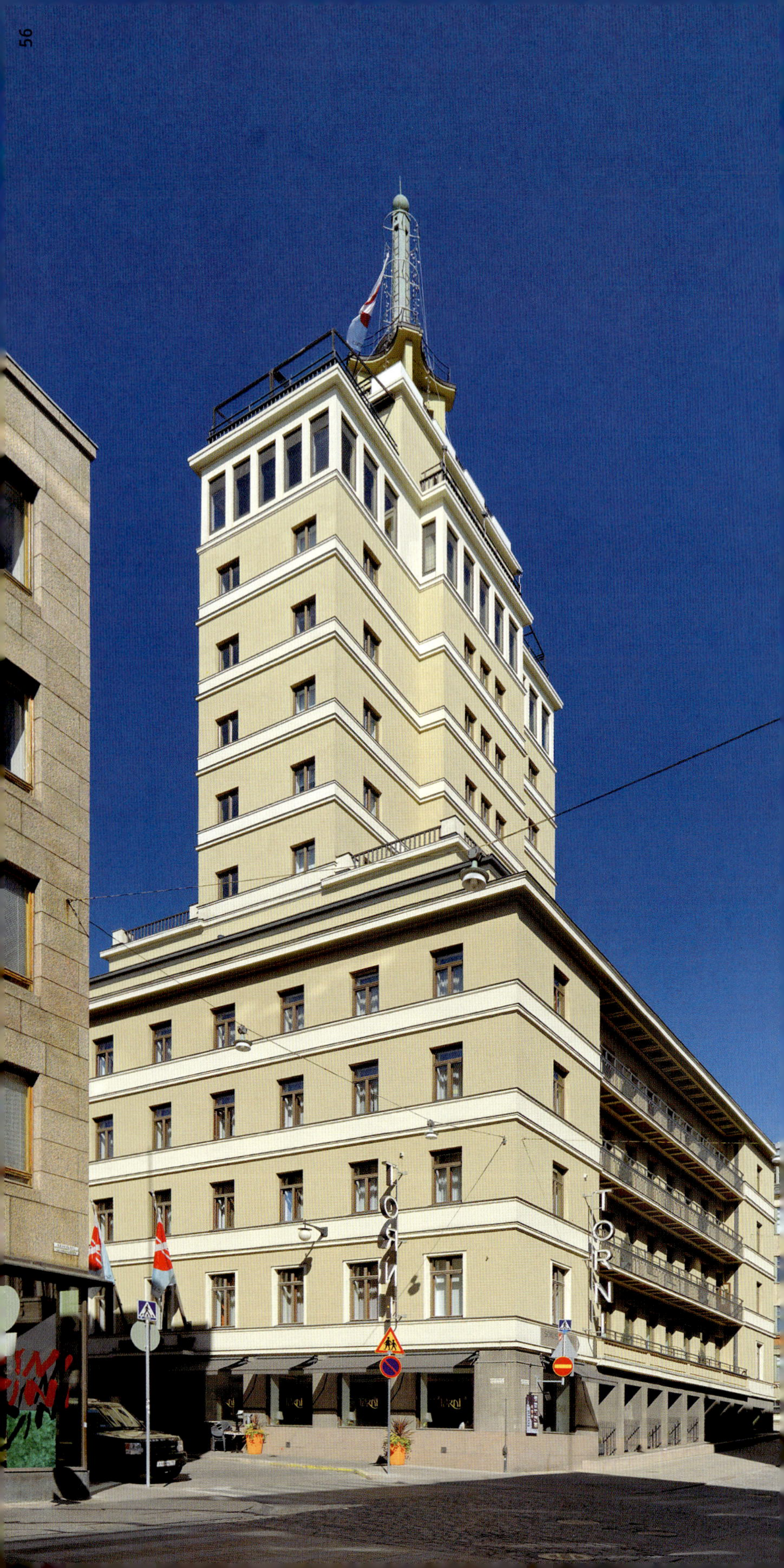
TORNI

Health and Welfare Ministry » C 039
Meritullinkatu 8
Pekka Helin, Peter Verhe
1999

The new Finnish Ministry of Health and Welfare stands on a corner lot in the Kruunuhaka residential neighborhood. The aim of the architects Pekka Helin, Peter Verhe was to make the new structure fit in with the existing buildings. The facades are clad in Finnish granite with stainless steel details. Narrow windows and strip windows break and divide the facades; the courtyard facades are white with brass windows. The large, tall foyer divides the building into two parts. This is where the main entrance from Mertullinkatu is located.

Hotel Torni « B 040
Yrjönkatu 26
Jung & Jung
1931

At its completion the 14-story Hotel Torni ("Tower"), designed by Jung & Jung, was the tallest skyscraper in Finland, it retained a status until 1976. In 2005 the huge building was extensively renovated and all rooms furnished in one of three styles: Art Deco, Art Nouveau and functionalist. The building now offers three conference rooms and four restaurants. During the World War II the Hotel Torni served as the air defense base and it was later used as the Allied headquarter. Located in the spire, the "Ateljee" bar offers views over the city.

Embassy of Norway ≫ B 041
Rehbinderintie 17
Eyvind Retzius and Svein Bjöland
1931

The Embassy of Norway is located in the district of Eira – an area well known for its Art Nouveau villas. Amid this ornate environment, the building of the diplomatic representation of Norway appears as a sober cube in the style of the of the sixties Modernism. The three-story building, designed by the Norwegian architects Eyvind Retzius and Svein Bjöland, has wooden facades with white strips. The building stands on a prominent corner lot at Rehbinderintietä and Hornintietä, thus dominating its residential neighbourhood.

Stora Enso Gutzeit Building ⌃ D 042
Kanavaranta 1
Alvar Aalto
1962

Because of its cuboid shape and white color the head office of the Stora Enso Gutzeit Building is nicknamed the "sugar cube". Stora is the biggest wood and pulp producer in Finland. The head office, located on a prominent water-side plot at the end of the Esplanade, right next to the Russian Orthodox cathedral and the port, is the culmination of a long series of designs which Alvar Aalto prepared and implemented for this company. Like all office buildings designed by Alvar Aalto, it has fine detailing and an interesting choice of materials. Some light fixtures and door handles were designed especially for this building. One of the four facades has no windows to allow an extension that was in fact never built. The 1897 Norrmén-house had to be demolished for the construction of the new headquarters. Above the regular grid of the facade there is a large rooftop terrace and a penthouse that houses the cafeteria. The square windows in wooden frames are set deep inside what was the white Carrara marble-clad facade. However, the Italian marble cracked in the harsh climate and was replaced by a stronger Portuguese one.

Embassy of Russia ⌄ D 043
Tehtaankatu 1b
E. S. Grebenshtshikov
1962

The former embassy of the Soviet Union today serves Russia. It is a good example of the soviet architecture of the early Fifties, the Stalin era. The giant freestanding building has gray granite facades over three storys, architecturally reminiscent of London's Buckingham Palace. The construction was financed by war reparations. The central main entrance is accentuated by a neo-classicist temple facade adorned with the "Hammer and sickle" symbol.

Embassy of Great Britain ⟲   `D 044`
Itäinen puistotie 17
Steven Quinlan
1990

Islamic Center ⚹ ⚻   `B 045`
Fredrikinkatu 33
Armas and Pauli Lehtinen
1961

The Embassy of Great Britain was built in Kaivopuisto 1990 next to the residence of the British Ambassador dating from 1918. To make way for the new postmodern building, the Baumgartner Villa, designed by finnish architect Lars Sonck in 1913, had to be demolished. When Britain bought the land in 1972 and pulled down the villa, citizens protested at the plans. The new chunky building has a Finnish stone clad facade and a central arched glass roof with interiors dominated by red granite. The four-story building contains offices and conference rooms. Parking with hydraulic lift, club room, canteen and kitchen are all located in the basement.

The Islamic Center of Helsinki is located at the corner of Fredrikinkatu and Uudenmaankatu. With its ribbon windows and exposed concrete surfaces it looks like a normal office building of its time. Only the crescent moon, a cupola on the roof and the Arabic calligraphy on the facade suggest the building's use. The center serves the Tatar community, who came from the Soviet Union in 1925 and founded the first Muslim community in Helsinki. Rent from the shop and office space on the lower floors partially funds the community. The mosque and the banquet hall are located on the fifth floor. The prayer room is oriented towards Mecca.

Metro Station Kamppi A 046
Urho Kekkosen katu 5b
HKP Architects
1983

Forum Shopping Center » A 047
Mannerheimintie 20
Kari Hyvärinen et al.
1985

The Kamppi metro station is well integrated into the shopping center of the same name that also includes a large bus terminal. Transport links are thus excellent. The subway station is the deepest in Finland lying 31 meters below ground and 15 meters below sea level. The pavilion-like ticket hall has skylights to let in natural daylight and the surfaces are covered with granite, bronze and glass. At right angles to the existing platform, a second station for later was built and in 2005 a new exit which leads directly into the Kamppi Center.

At its completion in 1985 the Forum Shopping Center, named after the 1952 Forum building which previously stood on the corner lot, was the largest of its kind in Finland. The design by the architects Kari Hyvärinen, Kaarlo Leppänen, Jaakko Suihkonen and Ilona Lehtinen won in an architectural competition in 1978. Inside the center, various shops and cafés flank a large central atrium, which occupies the entire height of the building. The existing Amos Anderson Art Museum was integrated into the shopping center.

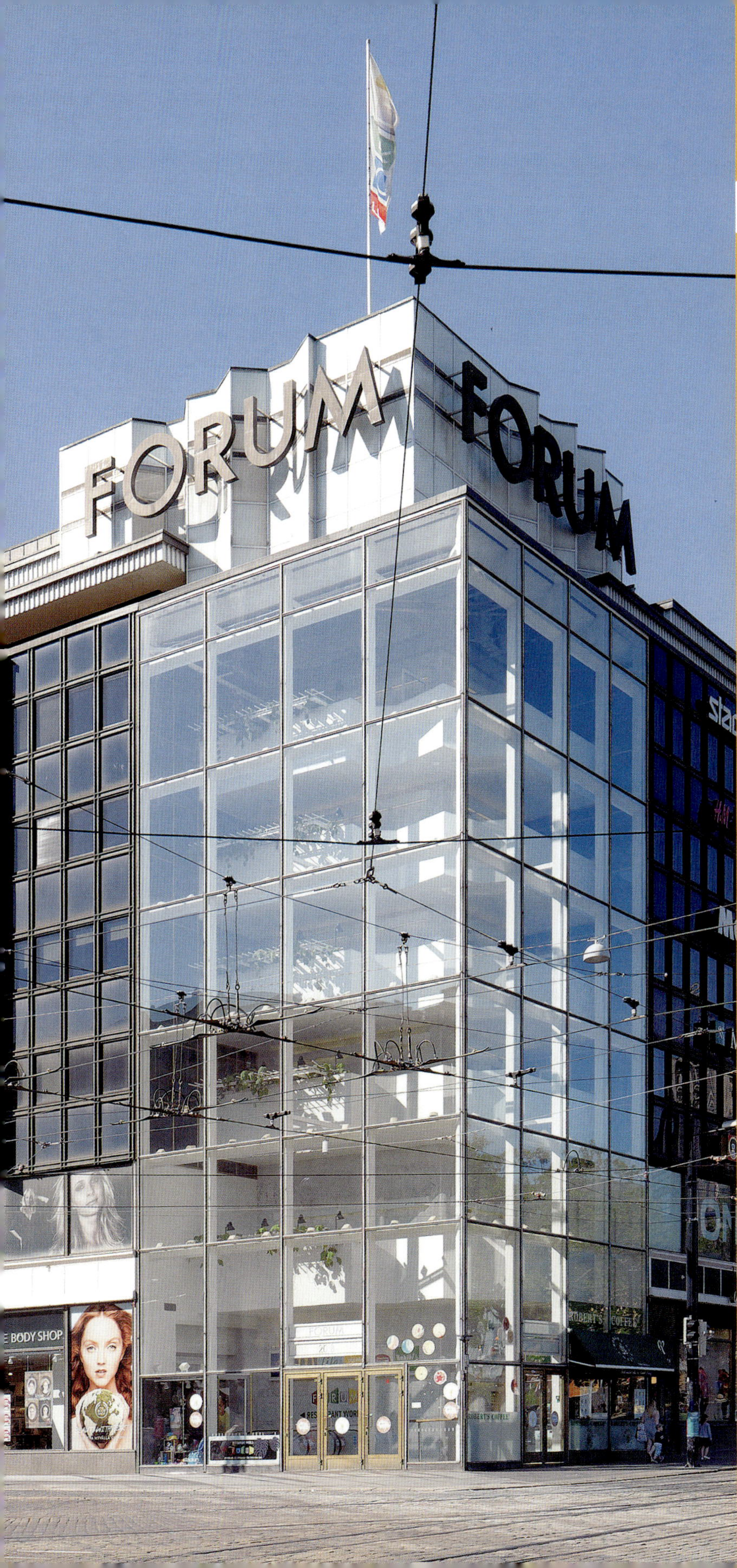
FORUM
FORUM
E BODY SHOP

WISA Hotel Pavilion ⌃ ⌄
Valkosaari Island
Pieta-Linda Auttila
2009

D 048

The WISA Hotel Pavilion on Valkosaari Island in the bay south of the city consists of two boxes with a connecting structure made of bent wooden slats. While one box contains the bedroom, the other one provides a living room. Both cubes have large windows at either ends that everyone is able to overlook the sea on one side and enjoy views of the city on the other. The curved wooden slats hold a small courtyard, which provides the lateral and upper battens protection against wind and weather through its curved design and produces an interesting play of light and shadow. The trim is made of pine, spruce and birch wood – the architect has used many different varieties of wood.

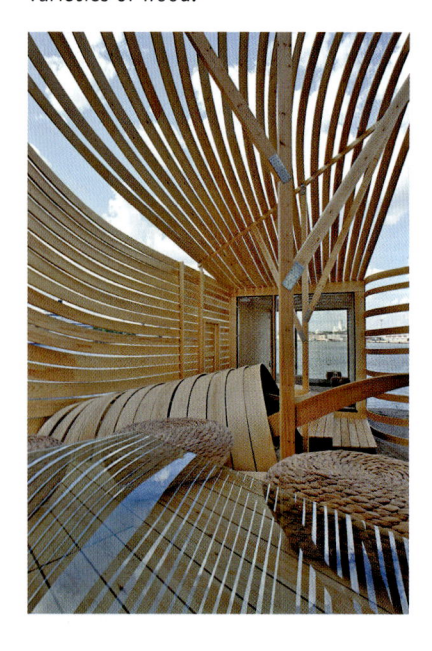

Mikael Agricola-Church ⌄
Tehtaankatu 23
Lars Sonck
1935

B 049

The church was named after founder of Finnish as a unified written language, Mikael Agricola, who also acted as a church reformer. Lars Sonck, the architect of the ecclesiastical building, has combined influences from Art Nouveau and Classicism in his striking design. The 106 meters high tower and the great hall visually extend the dimensions of the surrounding residential area. The spire is a 30 meters tall steel needle that reaches into the sky. The facades are of dark red brick and the prayer room is determined by a cross vault. The building shows little similarity with Lars Sonck's famous design for the Kallio Church. The church was renovated in 2004 by the Finnish architect Esa Piironen.

Hotel Simonkenttä A 050
Simonkatu 9
HKP Architects
2000

National Theater Extension C 051
Kaisankuja
Kaija and Heikki Sirén
1954

The design qualities of this hotel reflect the realm of urban design rather than architecture. The hotel covers a full city block and surrounds a rectangular courtyard. A high opening serves as an entrance towards Simonkatu. The eight to ten floors are placed on the sloping site in such a way that they harmonize with the heights of the surrounding buildings with the upper floors set back. The prominent north corner was emphasized in function and design: it contains the elevator lobby and restaurants on two levels, affording good views of Kamppi Square and the city and, in the opposite direction, into the interior of the hotel. The corner was accentuated with a round tower next to the vertical lift and a staircase illuminated by a billboard. The main entrance is through the courtyard and the roadside ground-floor space is reserved for commercial use. The roof terraces and porches offer access to a sauna, suites and a restaurant. The facades are made of stainless steel and glass with metallic green aluminum, natural stone and glass blocks. Towards the courtyard, the hotel has a perforated plaster facade.

The first theater building in Finland after the World War II was the extension to the National Theater that Onni Tarjanne had designed in 1902. The facade of the new building is made of glass and ceramic tiles that are reflected in the nearby water basin in Kaisaniemi Park. The extension contains a theater with 310 seats and a 153 meters big stage.

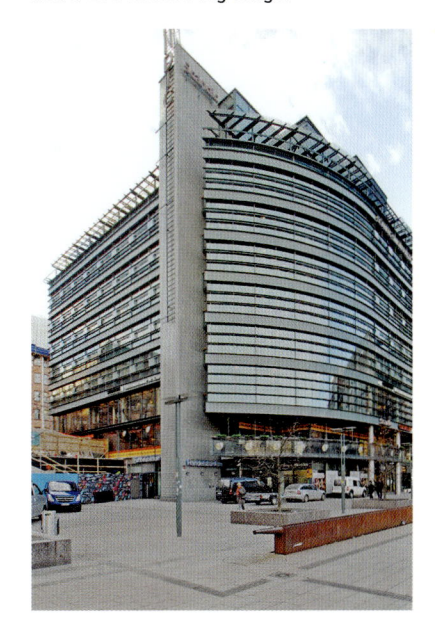

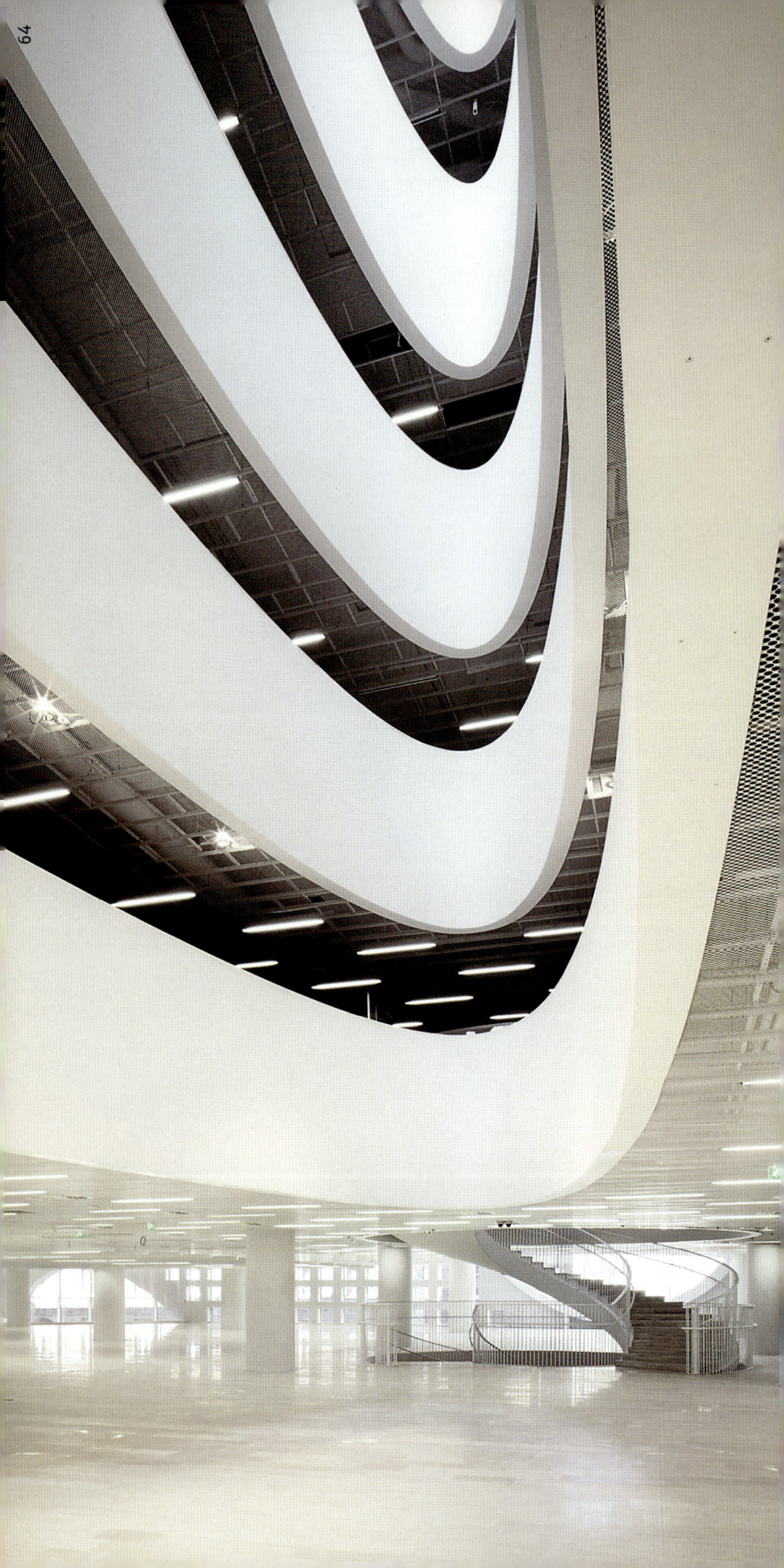

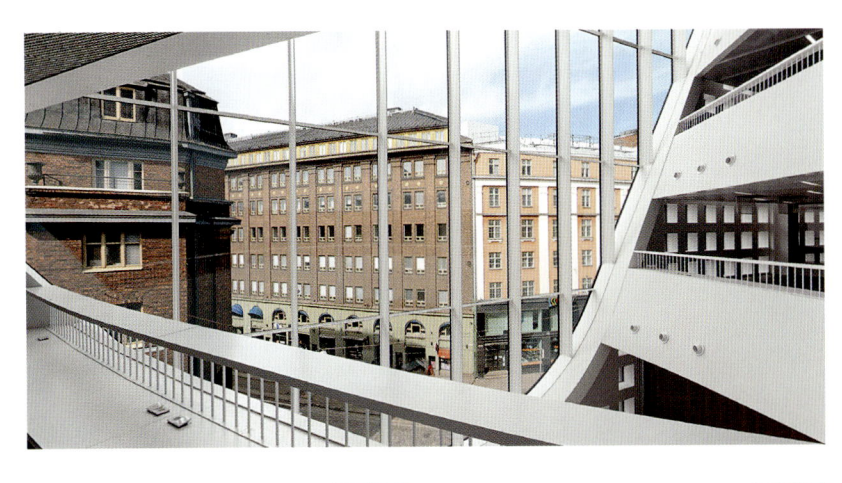

Library of the University `C 052`
Kaisaniemenkatu 5
Anttinen Oiva Architects
2012

The new Library of Helsinki's University contains the four libraries for law, theology, politics and a school library as well as a campus center and shops. Anttinen Oiva won the architectural design competition. His design fills an empty downtown lot with a strictly gridded brick facade, punctuated by large, parabola-shaped openings.

Aleksandria Learning Center ≽ `C 053`
Fabianinkatu 26
Aki Davidsson
2003

The Aleksandria Learning Center of the University of Helsinki is located in a courtyard behind a 1907 building by the architects Lindgren & Stenius. Although the building is listed, the wings were demolished and a new five-story structure added. It provides desks for students and a large library in the Kaisa building. The former residential building on the street is now used for the administration offices. Computer workstations are organized around a glass-roofed central hall and on the upper floors there are group work and seminar rooms. An underground passage connects the building with the lecture hall in the Porthania building and the Kaisa shopping center next door. The four upper floors offer 3,000 square feet of space. The facades are dominated by metal lamellas in bright primary colors.

Kiasma ⌂ ♪

Mannerheiminaukio 2
Steven Holl
1998

A 054

In 1993 Steven Holl was invited to participate in the architectural design competition for the construction of the new art museum in the city, against competing 514 European hopefuls. He was the only American participant and his scheme won. His design called "Kiasma" is the Finnisized form for the biological term "chiasm" (crossroads), alluding to the concept of the building. The museum houses the collection of Contemporary Art of the Finnish National Gallery over more than 9,000 square meters of exhibition space. It seeks to bring modern art close to a wide audience. The Kiasma has four floors with overlapping curved galleries. To the west there is a narrow shaft and to the east a trapezoid. At their interface there is an atrium with a long ramp leading to the upper floor. The floors are designed so that visitors can find their own way aroung the building and all rooms are naturally lit. The vaulted roof has narrow light slits cut into it. In the twilight the Kiasma glows mysteriously from within through its profile-glass facades. The facade consists of glass and hand-polished aluminum; the roof is of pre-oxydized zinc.

Sanomatalo ⌃
*Töölönlahdenkatu 2
Antti-Matti Siikala et al.
1999*

A 055

The new structure houses the editorial offices of the largest Finnish daily, the *Helsingin Sanomat*. It was completed in time for the 110th anniversary of the newspaper. About a thousand employees of the publishing house work inside. The Sanomatalo ("News House") is one of the first fully-glazed office buildings in Northern Europe. The northern sun illuminates the depth of the office floors well. Thanks to the long twilight hours, passers-by can watch the editors at work in the building that glows at night like a crystal. A secondary glass facade, a few feet away, was placed in a second layer for weather protection. The three lower floors contain an editorial office, a fitness room with sauna, a dozen conference rooms, a large auditorium and a canteen. The editorial, advertising and marketing departments, managerial and administrative offices are located in the top eight floors. The Sanomatalo building is square in plan with two diagonal paths cutting through. The publicly accessible ground and first floors are grouped around the 30 meter tall atrium containing an art gallery, a dozen shops, a restaurant, a design forum and various service counters. The northern corner is empty. The Builing of the *Helsingin Sanomat* is accessible to everyone. Glass elevators and sculptural stairs turn the vertical movement through the building into an exciting visual experience. The open floor plans are designed to encourage exchange and teamwork among staff. A special coating on the double facade reduces the summer-heat gains by allowing only one-fifth of natural sunlight into the building so that the workstations can lie directly in front of the facades. The Sanomatalo Building is in the mold tradition of representative newspaper buildings with high public visibility. Since the Twenties, architecture has seen interesting buildings of this type designed by some of the most famous architects.

F

075

062

Around the Center

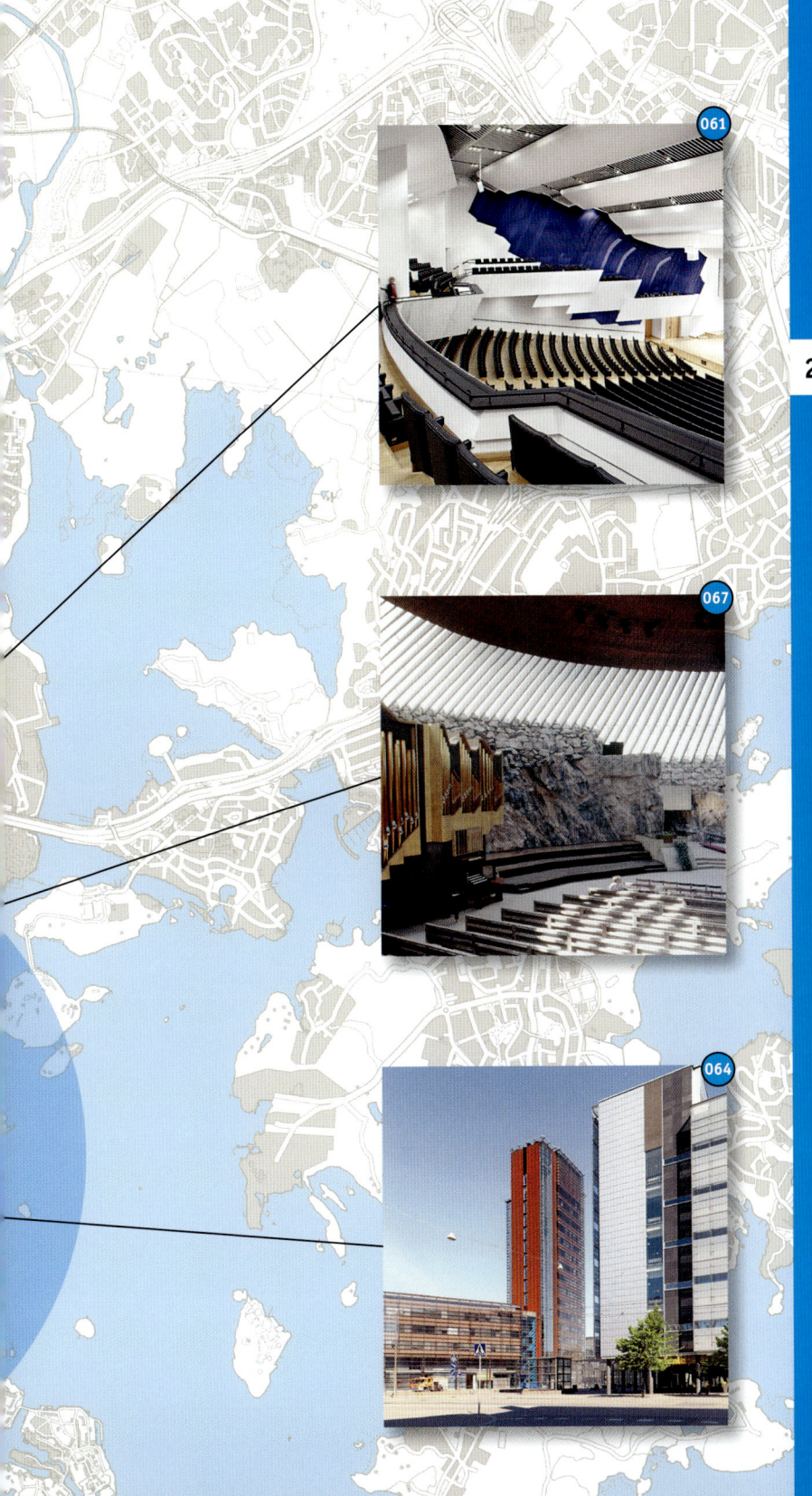

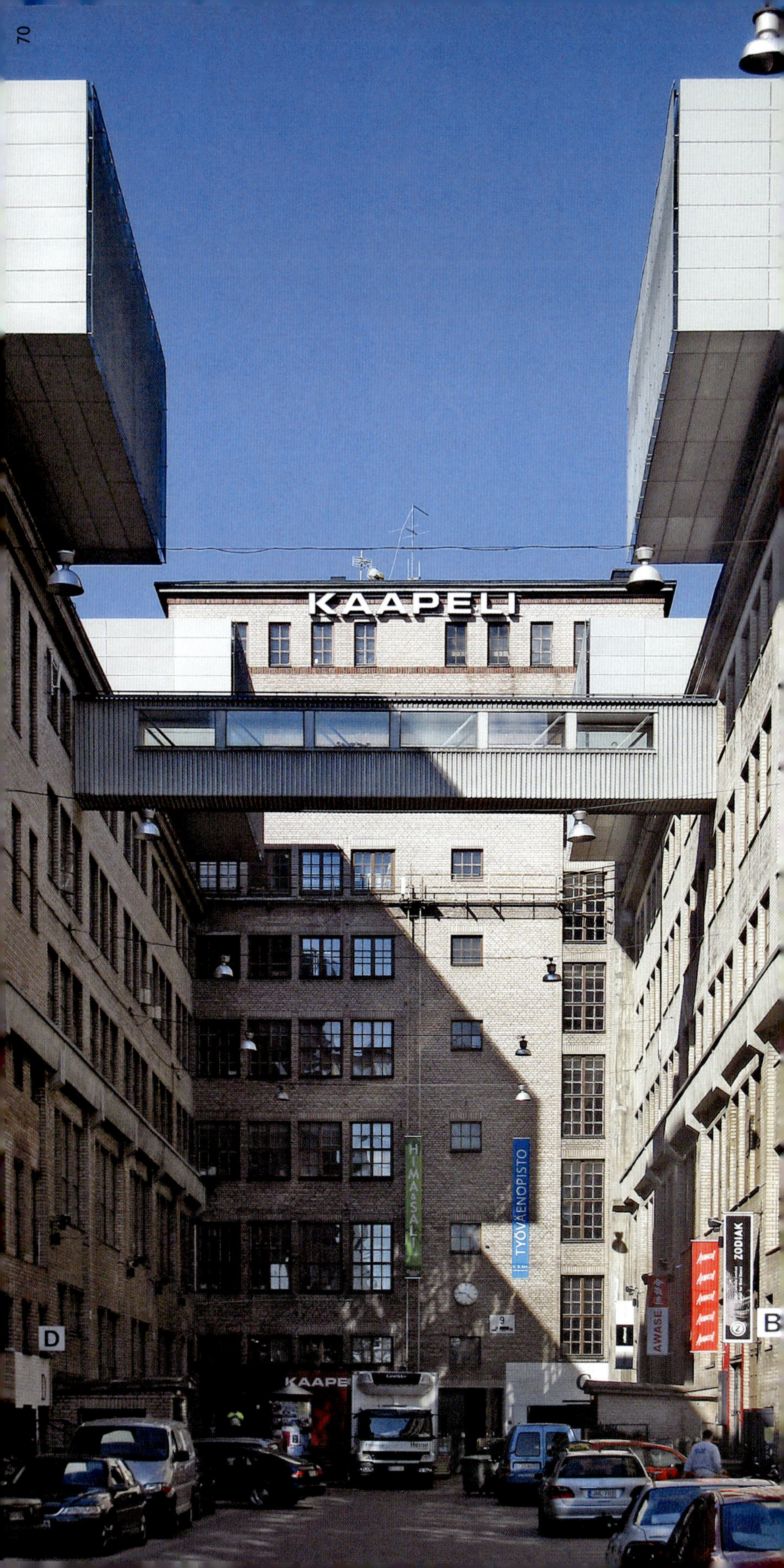
KAAPELI
TYÖVÄENOPISTO
ZODIAK
D
B

Former Nokia Cable Factory B 056
Tallberginkatu 1c
Wäino Gustaf Palmqvist
1943

Former Sinebrychoff Brewery ⌄ B 057
Bulevardi 42
Woldemar Baeckmann
1970

The "Kaapeli" building in Ruoholahti was built as a factory for the *Finnish Cable Works* which produced cables there from 1943 to 1987. The company was bought by *Finnish Rubber Works* in 1922 and went on to become a part of the Nokia conglomerate in 1967. The old factory was purchased by the City of Helsinki and converted into a cultural center. There are all types and sizes of event spaces for concerts, exhibitions and festivals. Three museums, 13 galleries, a dance theater, an art school and studio, rehearsal rooms, a radio transmitter and a cafeteria are also located in the former cable factory.

This building of the Sinebrychoff brewery closes the brewery premises towards Hietalahtentori Square. Like the older neighboring buildings, it has a facade of red brick. The closed ground floor contains the water filtering system. The two floors above housed the actual brewery, which can be viewed through large glass facades from the nearby square. Above that there is a canteen. The malt silos in the yard are six feet higher than the brewery and have smooth exposed concrete surfaces. Each year 800,000 hectoliters of beer were brewed here. The brewery was relocated to Kerava and the building was transformed.

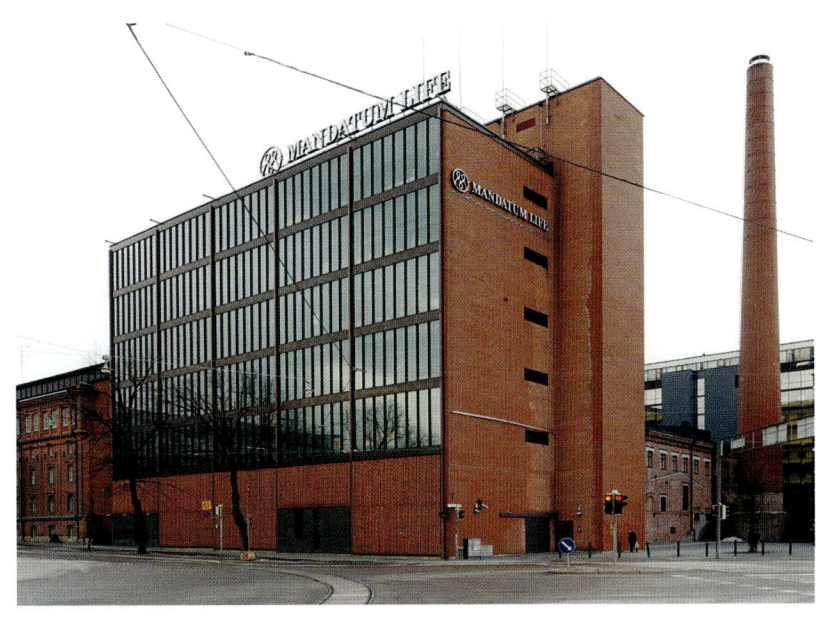

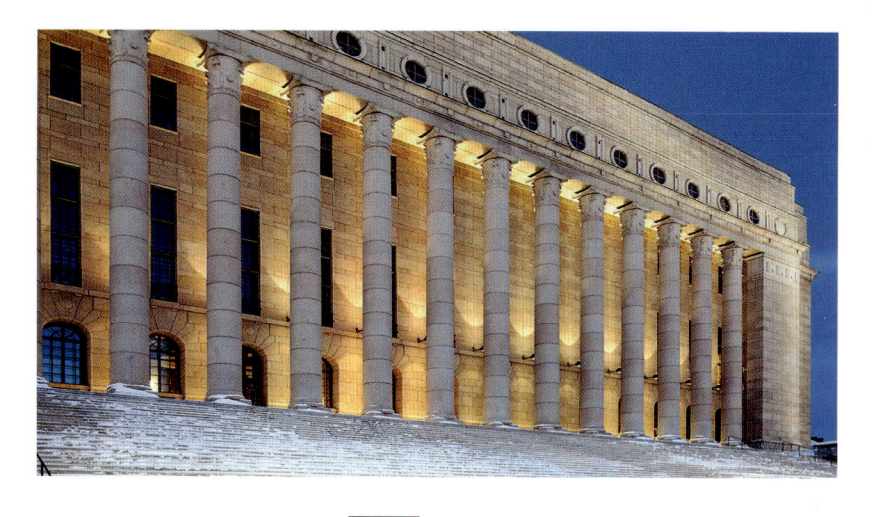

National Parliament
Mannerheimintie 302
Johan Sigfrid Sirén
1931

A 058

In 1923 a study concluded that the Arkadianmäki Hill in the Töölö District would be the best site for the construction of the new Finnish National Parliament. In 1924 the classic architectural design by Johan Sigfrid Sirén won an architectural design competition. The facades of the Parliament are covered with reddish Kalvola granite. Fourteen Corinthian columns adorn the front along Mannerheimintie. In his design Sirén combined elements of neo-classicism with modern features such as the simplified design of the monumental columns. White marble staircases and a paternoster connect the floors vertically. The basement houses the lobby, a meeting hall and the great "Hall of the State". The floor above contains the main foyer, a media room, information services, archives and dining rooms. The second floor is the main floor. It provides access to the public galleries of the plenary hall and a café. The floor above offers space for the information office and the press, the Protocol Office and several committee rooms. The fourth floor is reserved for political committees. On the top floor there are meeting and reception rooms.

73

2

Extension of the Parliament ⌃ A 059
Aurorankatu 6
LPR Architects
1978

Little Parliament A 060
Arkadiankatu 3
Pekka Helin
2004

The extension wing of the Finnish Parliament was designed by the Office LPR Architects. Its founders Ola Laiho, Mikko Pulkkinen and Raunio Ilpo had worked together since the Sixties. While the extension work was in progress, the same architects led to the Parliament itself being extensively refurbished. The new building is located behind the main parliament building. It is partially hidden behind a perimeter wall clad in the same granite that was used for the facades of the original parliament building. The ring-shaped new component has a brass facade. The low extension wing does not compete spatially with the older main building.

This expansion of the Parliament building called the "Pikkuparlamentti" (Little Parliament) provides office space for more than 100 delegates to the National Parliament of Finland. The building's name "Pikkuparlamentti" is derived from a restaurant that previously stood on the same site. The design by the architect Pekka Helin won in an architectural competition in 2000. A public "Kansalaisinfo" (Information center), the EU Secretariat of the Parliament, the office of the Ombudsman and some committee rooms are also to be found in the Little Parliament. For its construction local building materials such as birch, maple, pine and Finnish granite were used.

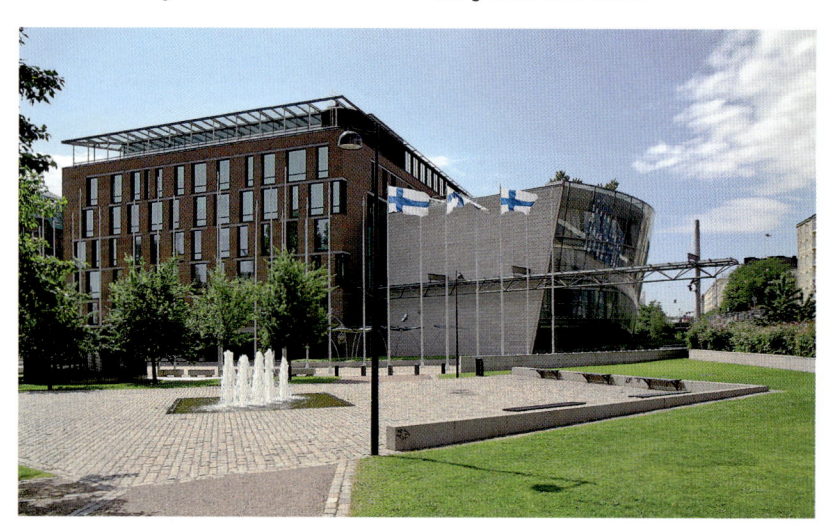

2

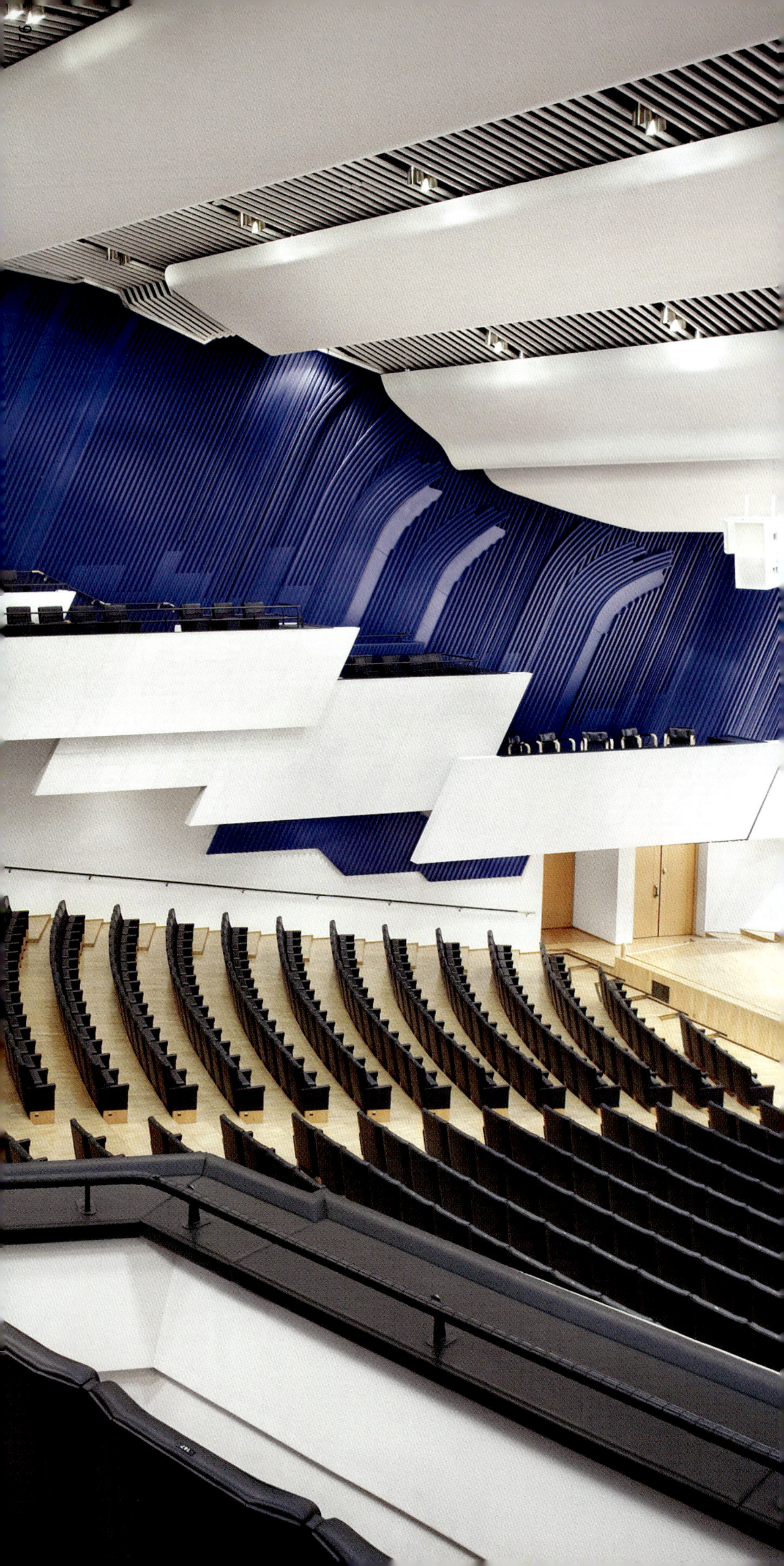

Finlandia Hall
Mannerheimintie 13e
Alvar Aalto
1971, 1975

A 061

The Finlandia Hall is the largest work by Alvar Aalto in Finland's capital and the only realized building from his city plan of 1961 which envisaged the establishment of a "pearl necklace" cultural buildings on the banks of the nearby lake. The hall is considered to be Finland's architectural icon. The concert hall area provides a large hall, a chamber music hall and a restaurant on the first floor while to the south there is a congress wing. The foyer overlooks the nearby lake. From here, two staircases lead up to the stands, one of which is visible through the glass. The horizontality of the facade towards Hesperianpuisto Park is broken only by the slanted stage tower of the great hall, which is covered with white marble and black granite. The facades were covered with thin slabs of Carrara marble, combined with copper roofs and teak window frames. The panels, however, proved too weak for the harsh northern climate and had to be replaced. The Italian marble is also to be found in the interiors, where it is combined with wood details and cobalt blue ceramic tile surfaces. A flat and wide staircase leads up to the large and smaller halls. The halls are determined by asymmetrical floor plans, balconies and walls made of marble and the acoustic panels. From the outset the acoustics were suboptimal, because the tiers create a pocket in which the sound is trapped. The floor plan is derived from the classical Greek typology. The southern congress wing was completed in 1975 as the second phase of construction in time for the OSCE Conference. Its great hall has 1,700 seats and the small one 340. Besides the convention hall holds 450–900 people. Currently, the car-parking spaces located on the lake side are being removed in favor of the addition of a new café and more conference rooms, and an underground garage is being created. After 2011, when the new concert hall with better acoustics next door was inaugurated, Finlandia Hall has had to reposition itself as a venue.

National Opera
Helsinginkatu 58
HKP Architects
1993

A 062

The National Opera is the leading opera in Finland. Opened in 1993, the Opera is located on Töölön Bay. The building itself has two auditoriums: the main theater with 1,350 seats, and a smaller hall with 300–500 seats. Regular opera performances began in Finland in 1873 with the founding of the Finnish opera by Karl Bergbom. Prior opera houses were only used temporarily and most singers were amateurs on tour. In 1956 the Finnish opera was taken over by a foundation and became the Finnish National Opera. Today, there are 30 full-time soloists, a 60-member choir, an orchestra with about 120 musicians and the ballet with 90 dancers. Overall, the opera is about 735 members strong. Every year the National Opera performs between four and six premieres including at least one world premiere of a Finnish opera. Access to the Opera Building is from the Mannerheiminitie through a sculpture courtyard. The street elevation does not reveal the building's full size, because the opera is partially inserted into the rolling hills on the site. The public areas enjoy views of the nearby Hesperia Park and Töölö Bay. The concert hall follows the traditional horseshoe typology and has three tiers.

House of Music
Mannerheimintie 13a
LPR Architects
2011

A 063

The new "Musiikitalo" or House of Music complements the architectural ensemble of the Finlandia Hall, the National Parliament and the Kiasma Museum of Contemporary Art which surround it. Its green copper facade establishes a relationship to the adjacent buildings and green spaces. The glass facades in the south and east provide views into the interior and enter into a dialogue with the building's neighbors. At its center there is the crater-shaped concert hall for 1,700 music-lovers. Its inner glass walls provide views from the foyer. The acoustic design is by Yasuhisa Toyota (Nagata Acoustics) from Japan. Besides the great music hall the center houses five smaller halls, rehearsal rooms for the Helsinki Philharmonic and the Radio Symphony Orchestras, as well as the headquarters of the Sibelius Academy.

Baltic Square Tower
Itämerentori 2
Pekka Helin
2000

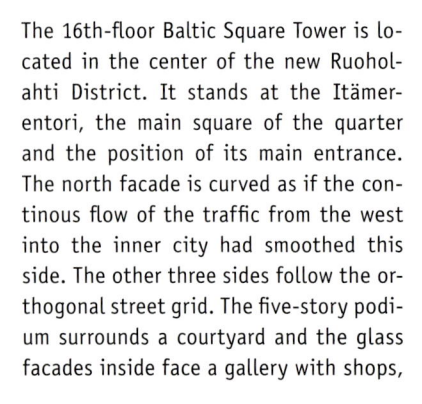

B 064

The 16th-floor Baltic Square Tower is located in the center of the new Ruoholahti District. It stands at the Itämerentori, the main square of the quarter and the position of its main entrance. The north facade is curved as if the continous flow of the traffic from the west into the inner city had smoothed this side. The other three sides follow the orthogonal street grid. The five-story podium surrounds a courtyard and the glass facades inside face a gallery with shops, cafés and a medical center, which is covered by a glass roof. The open plan office tower offers conference facilities and a sauna on its top floor. Some 600 people work in the building. In order to give the tower a slender silhouette, despite its relatively low height, when seen from the sea it has a distinctive shape. On the ground floor are the foyer and meeting rooms. The structure consists of a steel frame with precast concrete ceilings and the facades of glass and Cor-Ten steel. Its rusty color is reminiscent of the red brick buildings in Ruoholahti. The double glass facade insulates the building against noise and acts as a thermal buffer.

Nokia Research Center ⌃
Itämerenkatu 11–13
Tuomo Siitonen, Esko Valkama
1999

B 065

Nokia Research Center 2 ⌄
Itämerentori 9
Tuomo Siitonen, Esko Valkama
2000

B 066

The Research Center was designed by Tuomo Siitonen and Siitonen Architects and Esko Valkama Helin. Here, Nokia, the most famous of Finnish company developes the future of mobile communications. The center contains offices and laboratories. Architecturally, the design had to convey the communication among researchers, as well as allow for concentrated work and meet the client's requirements for secrecy. On each floor the building is divided into six, triangular "cells", of which two each share a break room with coffee bar. The triangular bulges on the north facade extend the length of the façade to accommodate more desks and subdivide the building. Each cell has a multi-functional, "empty" center. From the large atrium in the middle people can look through the glass facades into the surrounding offices. The lower floors contain visitor rooms, a cafeteria and the staff restaurant. The auditorium is designed as a stand alone building in the courtyard. The double skin facades have louvers at the top and are open at the bottom and the inner facade consists of wood frames and sandwich panels.

The extension of the Nokia Research Center is called "Deianeira". Its U-shape was a requirement of Helsinki's City Plan. A public footpath crosses the land, but the building is not accessible to the public for safety reasons. The staircase railing is made of glass, allowing natural light to penetrate the full height of the building and through walls of glass in the offices. The walls of the stairwell and the elevators are lined with oak panels. The vestibule is divided into two floors of combined offices with restrooms on the south facade. The street facade has an outer layer of sun-disc. The street arcade has steel slats made of perforated aluminum.

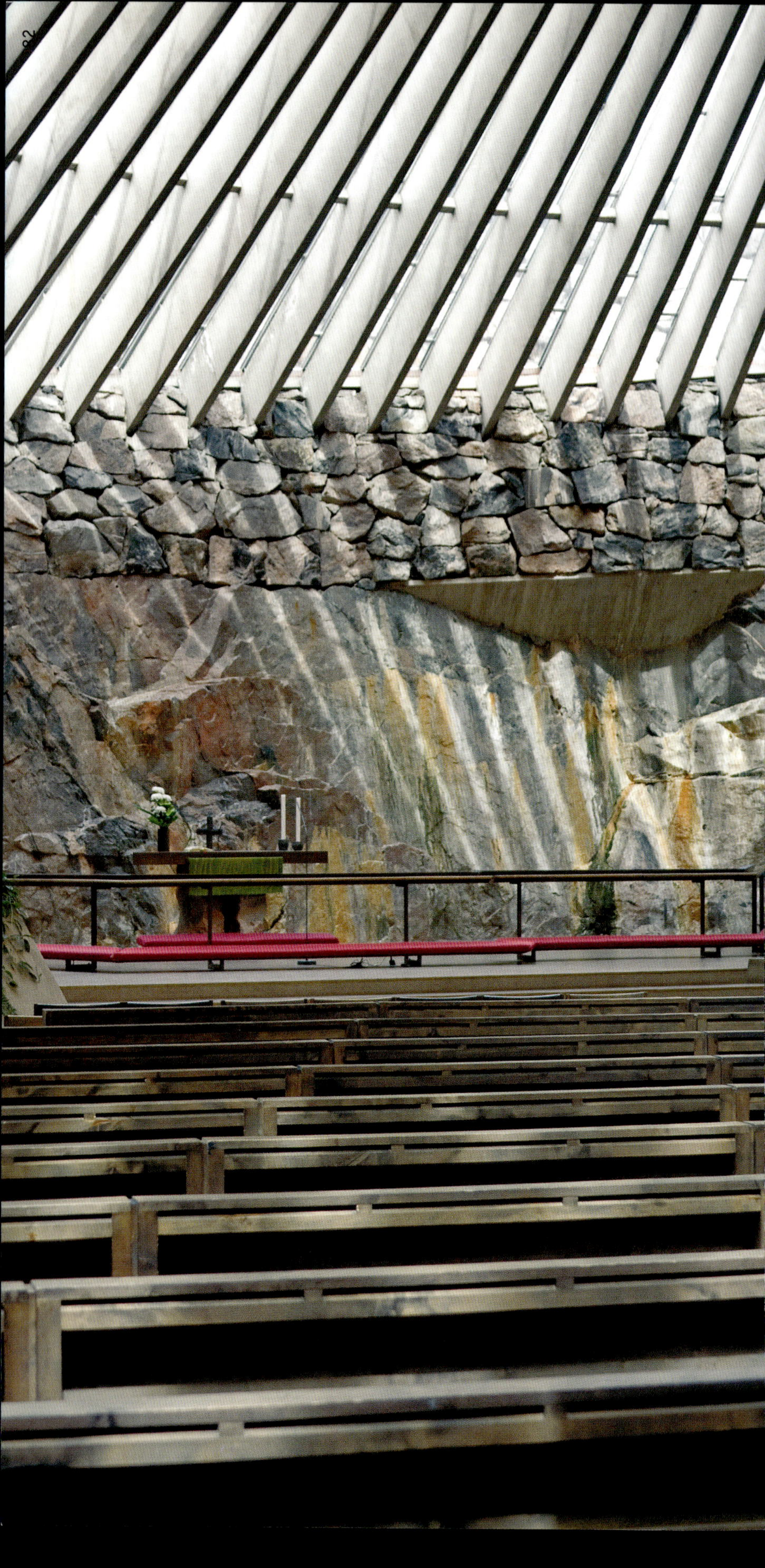

Temppeliaukio Church   A 067
Lutherinkatu 3
Timo and Tuomo Suomalainen
1969

Taidehalli (Art Gallery) ≈   A 068
Nervanderinkatu 3
Jarl Eklund, Hilding Eklund
1928

The Temppeliaukio Church in the Töölö District is an excellent example of Finnish architecture of the late Sixties. The church was designed by architects Timo and Tuomo Suomalainen and it is built largely into the granite rock on site. Daylight enters the church through a circular skylight that surrounds the 13 meters copper dome in the center. The 5 to 8 meters tall walls are made of rough-hewn rock. Besides the building's use for worship, the church also hosts concerts and it is a popular tourist attraction welcoming 500,000 visitors annually.

The design for the Taidehalli is the combined result of two architectural competitions: one was won by Jan Eklund, the other by Hilding Eklund. Like any other major gallery, the Taidehalli displays very different genres of art, from photography to installation art, and therefore must offer fairly neutral spaces. The Sculpture Hall receives daylight from above – from the side of the Painting Hall. The asymmetrical design of the Taidehalli breaks away from strict neo-classicism; the decoration is confined to the off-center entrance in the north.

Sandels Cultural Center ⌃
Sandelsinkatu 3
Juha Leiviskä
2007

A 069

Hanken School ⌐
Runeberginkatu 10
Kurt Simberg
1953

A 070

Like all designs by Juha Leiviskä and Rosemarie Schnitzler the architecture of the Sandels Cultural Center, too, is dominated by a staccato of sheer walls. The tall ground floor contains a large foyer and a bar overlooking the action on Töölöntori Square. The building is situated half up a hillside, so a gentle staircase leads to the upper level and down to a youth center. The upper floors contain classrooms. The glass meeting rooms at the ends of the corridors are visible through the facade facing the plaza.

Kurt Simberg won the 1948 architectural design competition for the new *Hanken* Swedish-speaking business school. The building is located directly next to the Finnish-speaking School of Economics. As a typical example of the brittle higher education architecture of the early Fifties, the Hanken School demonstrates simple volumes and a concrete skeleton structures. A large hall and the main auditorium form a hinge in the center of the school with the higher wings on both sides used for seminar rooms.

School of Economics ⌄
Runeberginkatu 14
Hugo Harmia et al.
1950

A 071

The Finnish-speaking business school is located in close proximity to its Swedish-speaking counterpart at the Runeberginkatu. Designed by the Finnish architects Hugo Harmia and Woldemar Baeckman, the school building, opened in 1950, consists of three components merging into itself, which can be seen, however, at a glance on the main facade. The auditoriums are situated in the main wing of the building directly behind the main entrance, which is marked by a large wall relief in the facade. The seminar rooms are located in the curved part, which also encloses a courtyard. The main auditorium with 770 seats for the students juts out from this bar-shaped element while the library sits quiet and separated on the top floor. The facades are made of yellow brick and the interiors of painted wood and brightly painted surfaces. The furniture of the individual classes are mostly made of lacquered wood. The exterior facades of the business school are marked by yellow straps. Diagonals are used in the design creating a consistent theme. In 1998 the Finnish trade school was renovated by the architects Kari and Tom Lindholm.

Salmisaari Power Station » B 072
Energiakatu
Hilding Ekelund et al.
1953, 1984

The two power plants in Salmisaari are higly visible landmarks at the western entrance to the city. Both coal-fired buildings have red brick facades, which are trimmed with white horizontal strips of concrete. The coal conveyer belts and chimneys and the staircases are detached. In the Eighties, the second power plant, designed by Timo Penttilä, Kai Lind and Heikki Saarela, was built with a similar formal vocabulary. Towards the sea the power plant is covered with black metal panels. Nowadays the main power plant in use is "Salmisaari B", while Block A generates heat and cold. Since 2004, the coal is stored in an underground coal bunker.

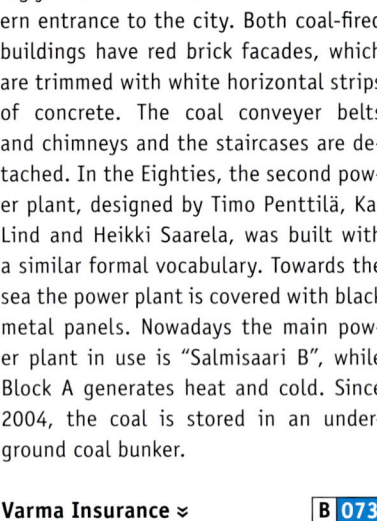

Varma Insurance ⩽ B 073
Salmisaarenranta 11
Tuomo Siitonen
2008

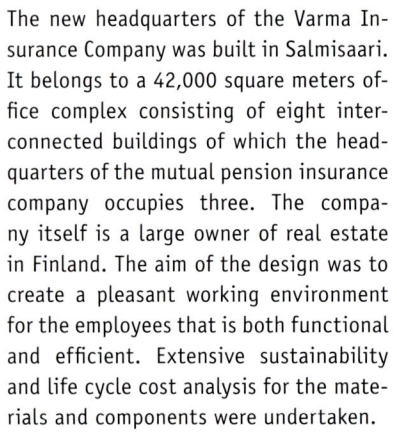

The new headquarters of the Varma Insurance Company was built in Salmisaari. It belongs to a 42,000 square meters office complex consisting of eight interconnected buildings of which the headquarters of the mutual pension insurance company occupies three. The company itself is a large owner of real estate in Finland. The aim of the design was to create a pleasant working environment for the employees that is both functional and efficient. Extensive sustainability and life cycle cost analysis for the materials and components were undertaken.

Supreme Court » B 074
Porkkalankatu 13
Väinö Vähäkallio, Tuomo Siitonen
1940, 2004

The former manufacturing plant and head office of the Alko state alcohol monopoly designed by Väinö Vähäkallio in 1940 was modified by Tuomo Siitonen to become the new seat of the Supreme Court of Finland in 2004. The massive dark red brick building dominates the western skyline of Helsinki. In the Nineties the alcohol production was moved to Rajamäki and the former factory floor is now used by the Supreme Court. In 2010, the court offices were completed in the former garage. The former head office has been carefully renovated.

87

2

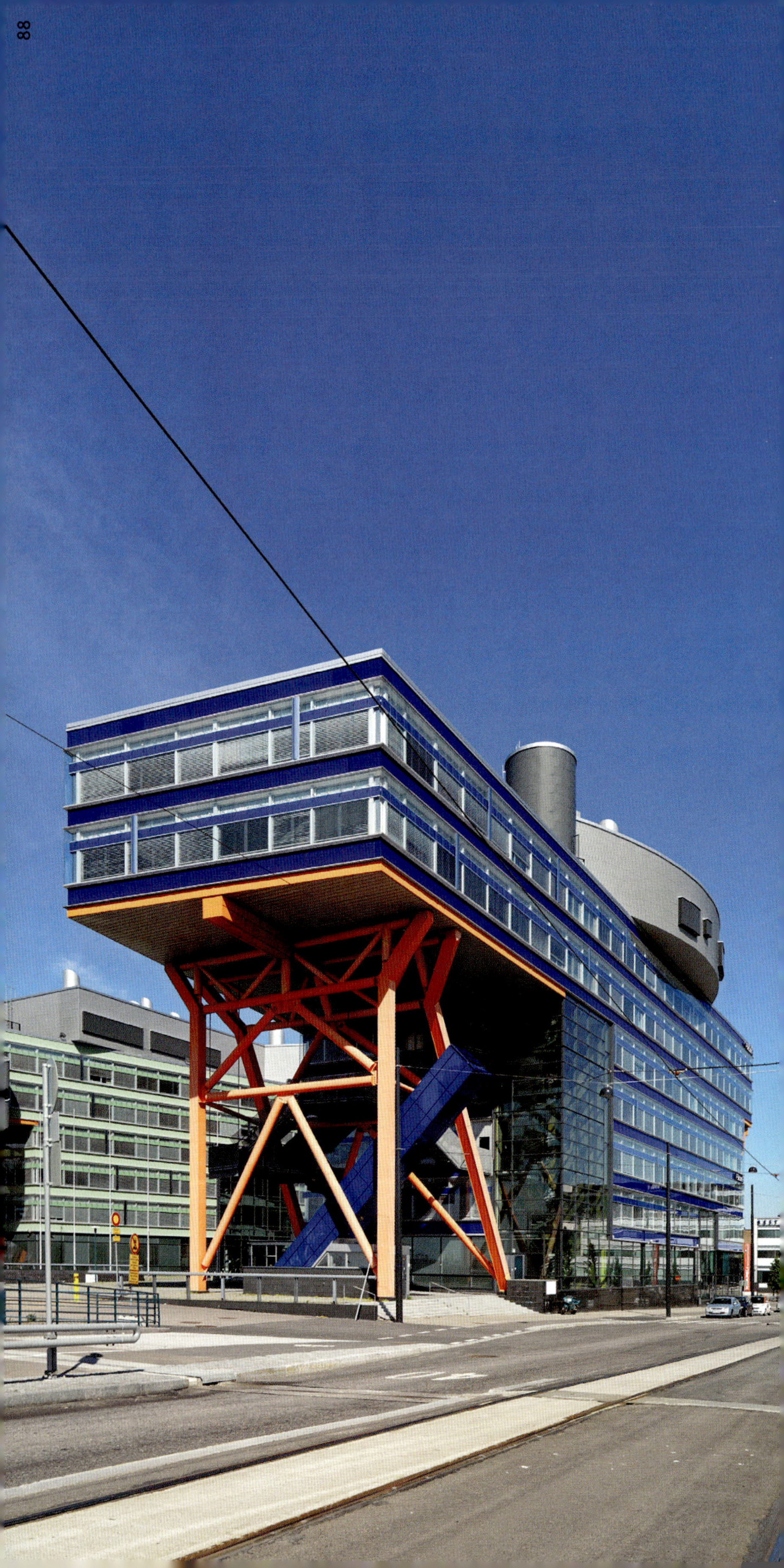

High-Tech Center | B 075
Tammasaarenkatu 1–7
Kai Wartiainen, Pöyry Architects
2001

Restaurant *Töölönranta* ⌃ | A 076
Helsinginkatu 56
Juha Leiviskä
1993

The High-Tech Center (HTC) is located on the banks of Ruoholahti. The five buildings were named after the ships of famous explorers: Columbus' *Nina*, *Pinta* and *Santa Maria*, Nordenskjöld Heyerdal's *Vega* and the *Kon-Tiki*. The colorful speculative office buildings, which cantilever towards the sea, are leased to more than 30 companies with more than 1,500 employees. The 36,000 square meters office space include large conference and meeting rooms. The basements of three of the five buildings are connected and contain an auditorium with 250 seats. Two adjacent conference rooms can also be interconnected.

The pavilion-like restaurant called "Töölönranta" fits sensitively into its plot on the edge of Töölö Bay. The red brick facade is a reference to the brick-clad sugar factory that once stood on the site. Towards the street the restaurant has a brick wall and towards the landscape park a large glass facade. A pergola follows the public footpath along the bay and also frames and shades the courtyard of the restaurant. The building with its green roof is pushed halfway into the hill on the property. Steel and wood surfaces characterize the interior, the kitchen and adjoining rooms have walls made of concrete.

G

083

086

Northwest

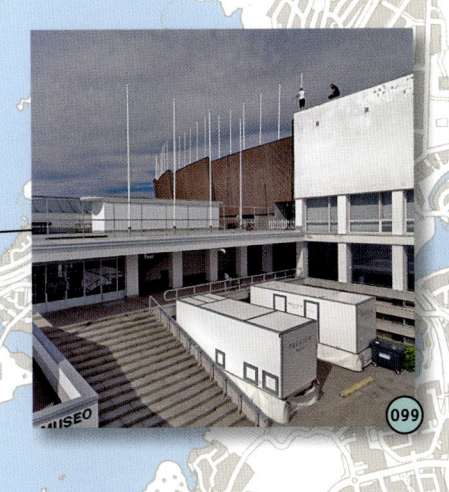

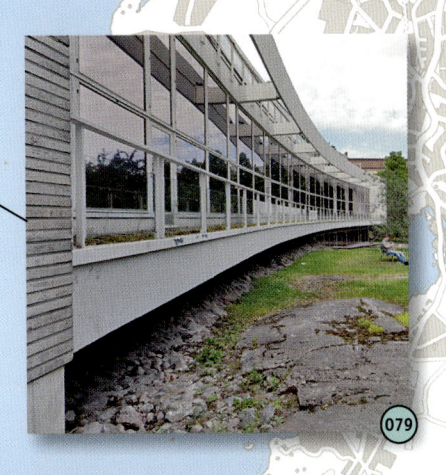

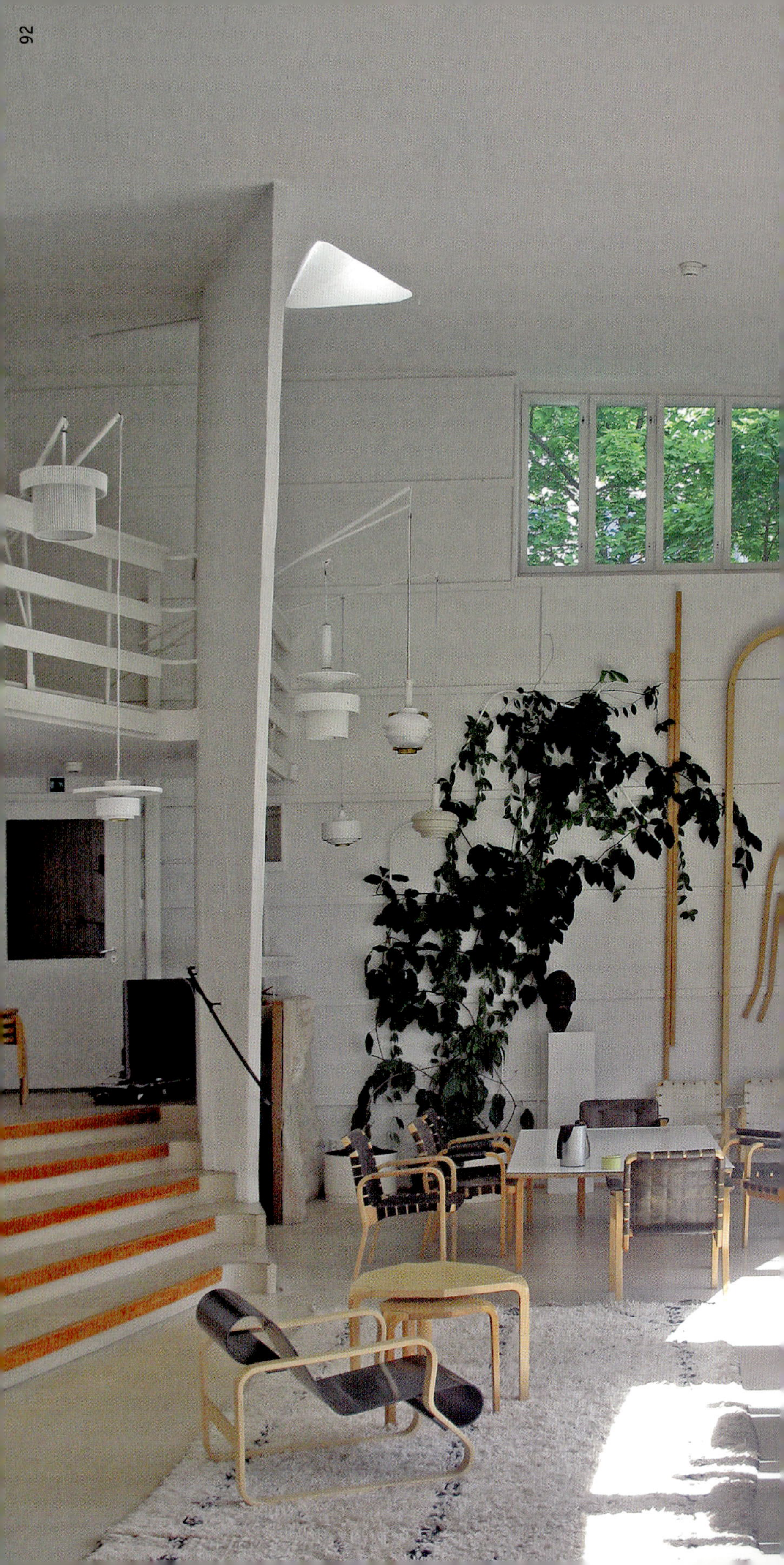

Aalto Studio L 077
Tiilimäki 20
Alvar Aalto
1955

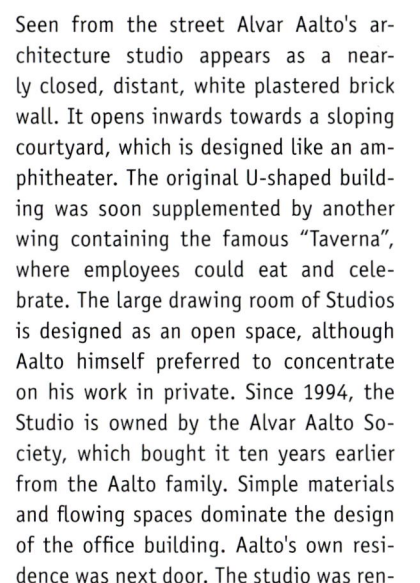

YLE Transmission Tower ⌄ L 078
Uutiskatu
Mikko Armanto
1983

Seen from the street Alvar Aalto's architecture studio appears as a nearly closed, distant, white plastered brick wall. It opens inwards towards a sloping courtyard, which is designed like an amphitheater. The original U-shaped building was soon supplemented by another wing containing the famous "Taverna", where employees could eat and celebrate. The large drawing room of Studios is designed as an open space, although Aalto himself preferred to concentrate on his work in private. Since 1994, the Studio is owned by the Alvar Aalto Society, which bought it ten years earlier from the Aalto family. Simple materials and flowing spaces dominate the design of the office building. Aalto's own residence was next door. The studio was renovated by Eric Adlercreutz in 2004.

The YLE Transmission Tower is a 146 meters high TV tower in West Pasila. It serves the state television YLE and is not publicly accessible. Because of its height it dominates the skyline of Pasila – the YLE Tower is the tallest freestanding tower in Helsinki and the second highest in the country.

Töölö Library ≈
Topeliuksenkatu 6
Aarne Ervi
1970

A 079

At the north end of Topelius Park lies Töölö Library which was built in 1970 after a design by Aarne Ervi. The building is curved in plan and quite closed towards the main entrance at the street, but opens up towards the south and the park with a large glass facade. The landscape architecture supports the impression that the building seems to grow out of the site and its topography. The newspaper reading room and children's library on the ground floor have direct access to the park. The main floor contains the large reading room. On the floor above, in the recessed attic, the music room and a cafeteria are to be found.

Töölö Church ≈
Topeliuksenkatu 4
Hilding Ekelund
1930

A 080

This church forms the southern end and focal point of Topelius Park. The main entrance from the park is located directly under the tower, which culminates in an open belfry. On the ground floor of the church there is a wing for confirmation classes and social spaces. The baptismal and wedding chapels are located on the floor above. The rooms are decorated in light blue and pink, a typical choice for the architecture of the Nordic Neo-Classicism of the late Twenties.

Motor Battalion Barracks ⌃   A 081
Mechelininkatu 23
Martta Martikainen
1935

Exhibition Hall ⌄   A 082
Paavo Nurmen kuja 1c
Aarne Hytönen et al.
1935

The barracks of the Helsinki Motor and Transport Battalion is typical of the functionalist formal language of the German "Neue Sachlichkeit". It was designed by the young architect Martta Martikainen, who shaped the architecture of the Finnish military of her times. The barracks of the Motor and Transport Battalion stand on a prominent street corner, accentuated with a flagpole and rounded corners. The staircase has vertical band windows and the interiors contain valuable built-in furniture. Originally the building provided space for the soldiers and their vehicles; nowadays it is used only for civilian purposes.

The multi-functional exhibition hall with its barrel roof was built in preparation for hosting the 1940 Summer Olympic Games. At the time of construction, it offered the largest indoor space in the country. During the Olympics the competitions in gymnastics, wrestling, boxing, weightlifting and basketball were held here. The hall is surrounded on three sides by galleries with a restaurant over the main entrance on the fourth. In 1941 an extension was added and in 1950 a second, smaller hall. Since the completion of the exhibition grounds in Pasila the two halls are used mainly for sporting events, concerts and exhibitions.

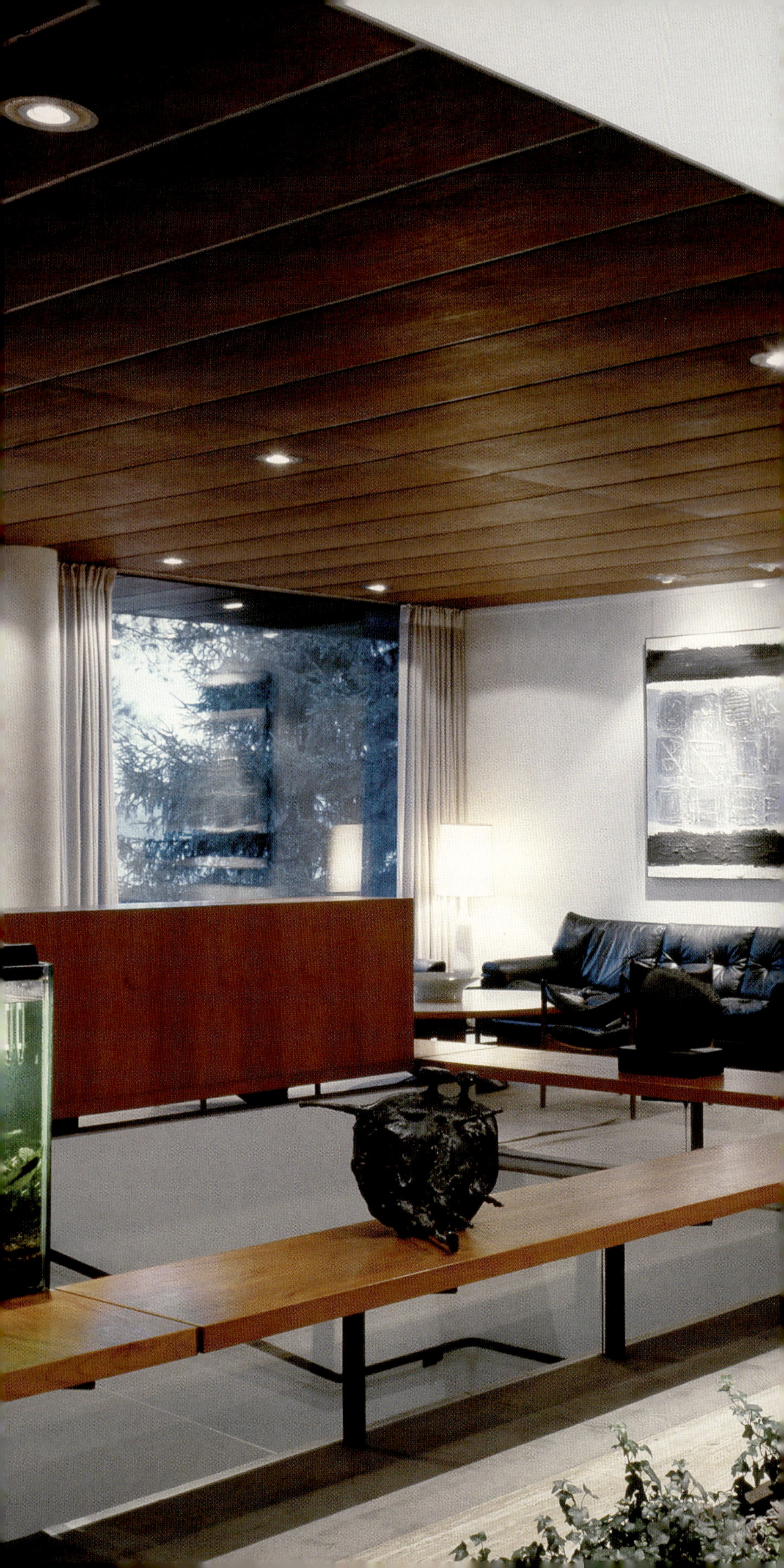

L 083

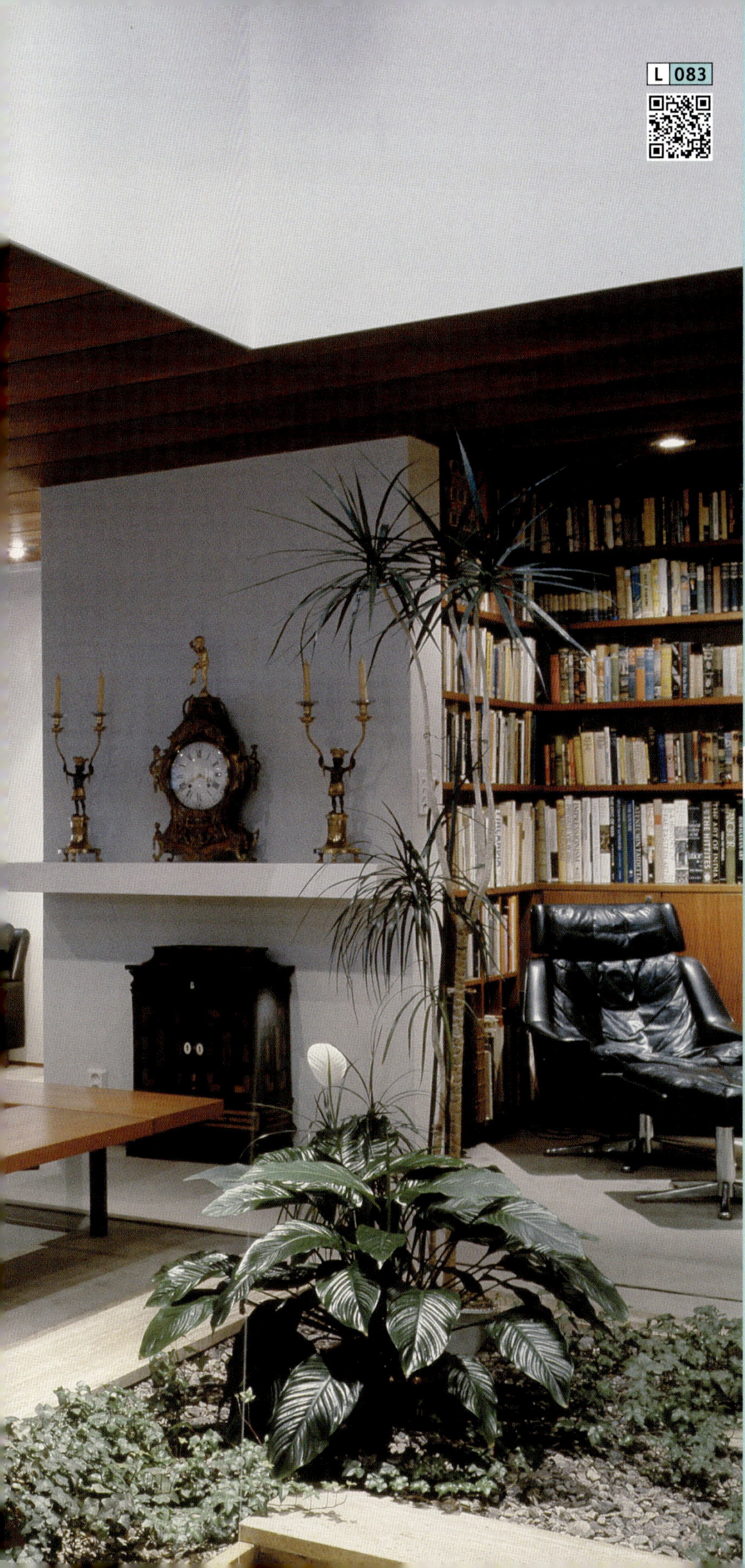

Didrichsen Art Museum
Kuusilahdenkuja 1
Viljo Revell
1959

L 083

The both art collectors Marie-Louise and Gunnar Didrichsen have accumulated an impressive collection of 20th-century Finnish art supplemented with works by international artists such as Pablo Picasso, Wassily Kandinsky, Joan Miró, Henry Moore, Alberto Giacometti and Jean Arp. The basement of the villa contains the only significant Finnish collection of pre-Columbian American art, as well as an Asian collection with a focus on Chinese art as well as the Shang and Ming Dynasties. 1965 an extension wing was built for the art collection. The cozy museum mixes architecture, art and nature. The windows offer excellent views of the surrounding garden, which is decorated with a sculpture by Henry Moore. The architect of the villa, Viljo Revell, had worked for Alvar Aalto before, where he had "learned the humble and humanistic version of modernism" (according to the museum). In the Fifties Revell tended to a more rigorous rationalism, inspired by Le Corbusier and British Brutalism.

National Pension Fund ⌄　　A 084
Nordenskiöldinkatu 12
Alvar Aalto
1956

German Embassy ⌃　　L 085
Krogiuksentie 4
Juha Leiviskä
1993

To make a large office building such as the headquarters of the National Pension Fund appear less overwhelming, the building's architect, Alvar Aalto, subdivided its mass into several sections. The band facades have alternating stripes of red brick, copper and black granite. Each office has at least one openable window. Walls and pillars are covered with ceramic tiles in different colors from the Arabia factory, which is located nearby. Alvar Aalto also designed light fixtures, sound-absorbing walls, modern radiators and furniture especially for this building. The small library is reminiscent of Alvar Aalto's library in Viipuri.

The design of the Finnish architect Juha Leiviskä won in the 1986 competition for the construction of the German Embassy. The building was intended to serve the Federal Republic, but it was completed only after German reunification. The architect's design is characterized by a high degree of empathy for the landscape and its topography. The segmentation of the Jura limestone-clad building literally and visually breaks down the large volume, while a yard inside frames the view to Seurasaari – an island where the Building Conservation Center is situated. The guest rooms follow a sequence of spaces of differing heights.

Building Conservation Center ⌃ L 086
Seurasaari Museum Island
Seppo Häkli
2009

The open-air museum on Seurasaari Island is home to 87 historic buildings dating from the 17th to the 20th centuries. The shape of the new Building Conservation Center was borrowed from vernacular farms where buildings and fencing create an enclosed courtyard that is protected from wild animals. The main building at the center is used to carry out conservation work for the buildings in the open-air museum and contains a wood workshop. The courtyard is divided into an area for equipment and one for presentations, which is framed by the workshops. The long pent roofs facilitate the removal of snow in winter. The structure has double columns made of solid wood and a cantilevered roof supported by glulam beams. The tarred pine walls of the storage room contrast with the bright pine of the main building. The center was commissioned by the National Monument Office. Its design is modern, but the materials and craftsmanship are traditional.

Former Boarding House ⬥ L 087
Hollantilaisentie 11
Eliel Saarinen
1919

YLE Broadcasting Company ⬥ L 088
Radiokatu 5
Ilmo Valjakka
1993

This Art Nouveau building, designed by Eliel Saarinen, stands at the western end of Munkkiniemi garden city, which Saarinen planned in the west of Helsinki in the first decades of the 20th century. It is one of the few parts of the architect's urban development plan ever built, it was formerly designed as a boarding house for 100 hundred guests to attract wealthy clients to the area, but went bankrupt and now serves as the Administrative Development Agency, a state educational institution. The building was nationalized in 1923 and used as a cadet school until 1940 and then, until 1973, as the headquarters of the Finnish Air Force. It has been extensively renovated. The large entrance hall, lounge and dining room in the tower are the three most important rooms in the building.

The headquarters of the national Finnish Radio- and TV station YLE was built on a granite hill in Pasila. The main facade is clad in granite panels with horizontal joints made of stainless steel. A glazed atrium opens onto the street while rooms with elliptical shapes form an internal road. The building is also known as "Iso paja" (big workshop). It is the culmination of a series of office buildings that frame the studio complex in West Pasila along the railroad. The large glass hall, two towers and cubes are arranged like a collage. From the "News Square", an axis with a restaurant on one side and an auditorium and studio on the other leads to a water basin. More than 600 people work in the building. The offices are located in the upper floors and are arranged around small courtyards.

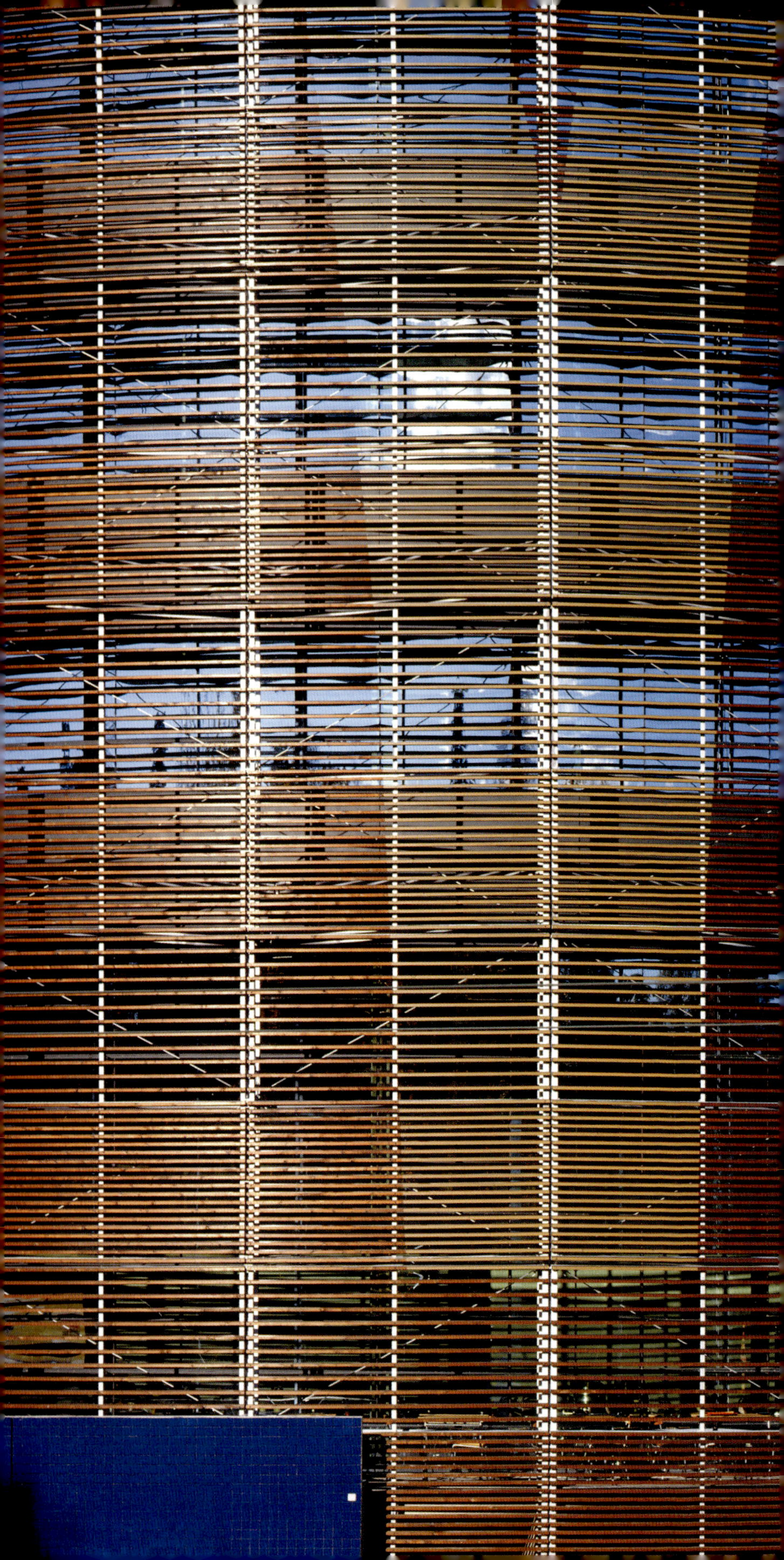

McDonald's Headquarters L 089
Paciuksenkatu 29
Mikko Heikkinen, Marko Kumon
1997

The main building of McDonald's in Finland is circular in plan and thus similar to the tower of a city wall. Easily visible from all directions, it serves as an end-point for the nearby new residential neighborhood planning from the Eighties. The building includes a fast-food restaurant, a staff training center and offices. Continuous band windows provide excellent views of the landscape from anywhere in the building. On the sunny southern side a wooden trellis is made of coated spruce and mounted on a steel structure. The restaurant recalls the atmosphere of the Fifties and the first McDonald's restaurants – designed by American architect Stanley Meston. The picture on the wall of the restaurant by Pekka Mannermaa celebrates the classic McDonald's, which was founded in 1954 in Des Plaines, Illinois. Glass walls allow customers to see into the kitchen, as was customary in the Fifties. The client did not require that the design would be recognizable as a standard company's building but the inclusion of the logo shows the power of the sign. Above a soundproof wall, covered with blue glazed tiles, a six meters high yellow "M" was attached to a perforated, hollow construction, which is illuminated from within so that the shadow falls on the wooden trellis. Observers register the sign as a function of their position, the weather and light conditions. Overall, the building offers 3,580 square meters of space.

Postal Service Headquarters « L 090
Postintaival 7
Lahdelma & Mahlamäki
2003

The Finnish post office decided to relocate its headquarters to Pasila. The architects Lahdelma & Mahlamäki have designed the striking blue building in a semi-circular plan in order not to obscure views from of the old building into the surrounding nature. In front of the blue aluminum panels of the facade are aluminum fins.

National Library of Medicine L 091
Haartmaninkatu 4
Olli-Pekka Jokela
1998

The new building that houses the library of the University of Helsinki's Faculty of Medicine was designed by Olli-Pekka Jokela, whose entry won the invited architectural competition held in 1995. The tall building comprises 4,700 square meters of gross floor area and opened in 1998. Both the exterior and the interior are characterized by a combination of white rendering and glass, with walls of soundproof glass protecting the reading room from the noise of the adjacent street. A skylight provides the area around the information counter on the ground floor with ample natural light. The interior decoration is based on various shades of gray that form a calm and attractive color scheme. The bookshelves are arranged in a clear layout and the books are organized alphabetically. A staircase separates the reading rooms along the street front from the shelf area. Periodicals and professional journals are housed separately in a cozy room furnished with a coffee machine and comfortable seating. Five shelf miles of books, 50 computers, 110 reading desks and a lecture room provide students and researchers with all necessary facilities to obtain medical and health-related information.

Meilahti School L 092
Jalavatie 6
Viljo Revell, Osmo Sipari
1953

The Meilahti School is a two-story, red brick building with a curved floor plan, which forms a semi-protected courtyard. The large classroom windows open onto this central school yard to the south. The rear facades are almost closed. To the left and right-hand sides of the main entrance, four class rooms are arranged down a long corridor. The gymnasium and cafeteria are located in the north wing. The staircase and the sports hall have facades made of glass blocks. The administration offices and break room are upstairs.

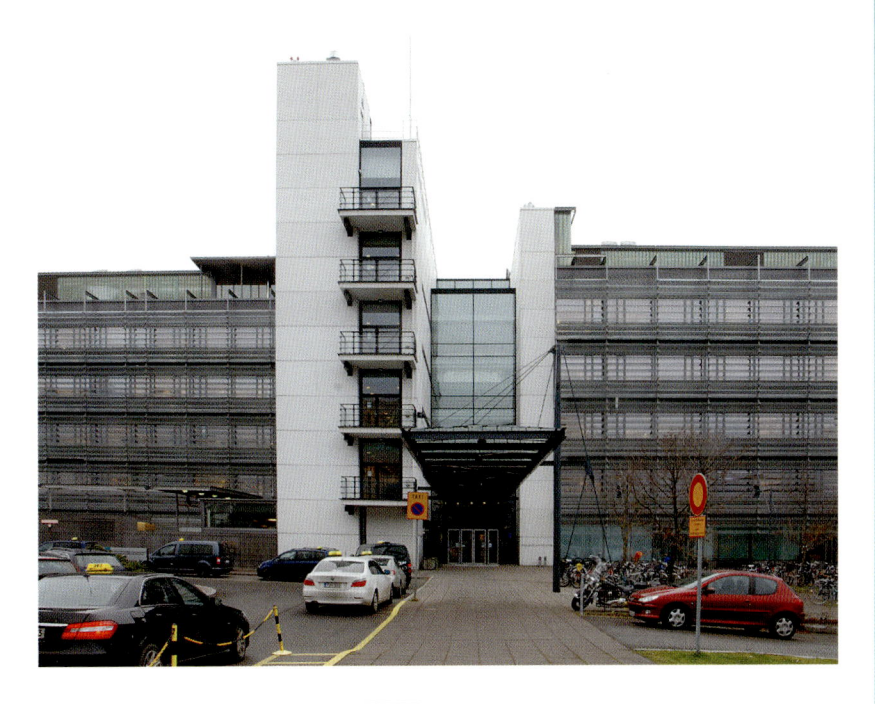

Biomedicum ⌃
Haartmaninkatu 8
Kristian Gullichsen et al.
2001

L 093

The six-story Biomedicum is a university hospital and one of the leading centers for medical research and teaching in Finland. Its elegant, white plaster cube is reminiscent of Alavar Aalto's modernistic health care designs. On 22,000 square meters of space, the Biomedicum offers research for the University of Helsinki in basic and clinical sciences. A range of other research institutes and companies also use the building. As the heart of Meilahti Campus, the Biomedicum specializes in six research areas: cardiovascular, developmental and reproductive biology; molecular medicine, cancer biology, neuroscience and drug development. The aim of the building's design is to keep the floor plans easily adaptable to meet the future needs of researchers, students and employees and foster interaction between laboratory research and the use of the facilities. Large-scale facilities such as auditoriums and conference rooms are used for meetings, teaching, conferences, commercial or scientific training, seminars, symposia and congresses. Elegant reception rooms create an excellent setting for employees. The Biomedicum is connected by a tunnel network to other facilities on Meilahti Campus.

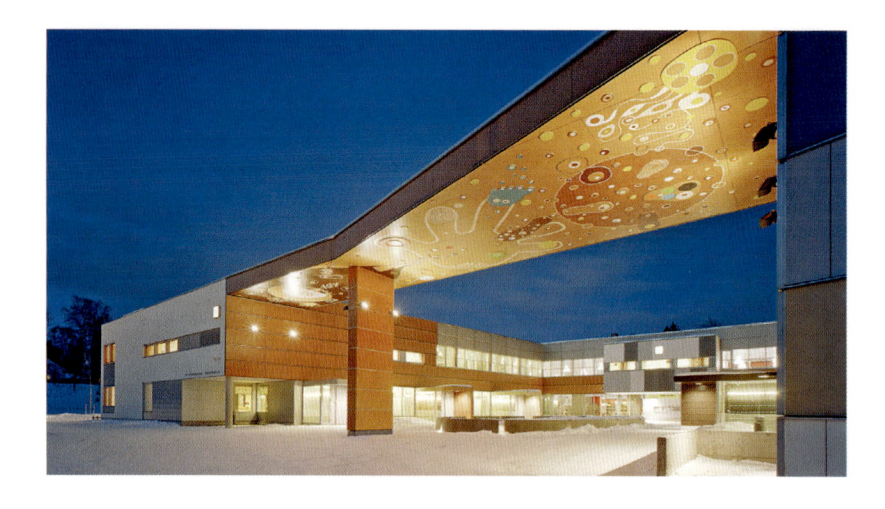

Hiidenkivi School ≈ ↑   M 094
Rajatie 7
Seppo Häkli
2005

Soininen School ≈   M 095
Kenttäpolku 3
Ilmari Lahdelma
1997

This large school seems flatter than it really is because it is incised on one side. The east facade, which faces the nearby residential area, matches the neighboring buildings in color and proportion. A central courtyard is flanked by a large pergola, the underside of which is decorated with a great work of art. Five entrances lead from the courtyard to the classrooms. The rooms for the lower grades are upstairs and lead to a second courtyard. The classrooms for the age groups 1–9 are divided into compartments, each organized around a foyer, called the "Apila" (clover leaf). Each *clover leaf* contains four classrooms, a teachers' and a storage room. The school offers four support groups and a preparatory school for immigrants.

The Soininen Elementary School in northeast of Helsinki is named after the Finnish politican and teacher Mikael Soininen. In the architectural competition held in 1994 a design called "City of Children" by Ilmari Lahdelma won first prize. The classrooms are divided into three "home areas" with their own entrances. Each contains four normal classes and one for mentally handicapped-children. The rooms can be connected to form one large hall. The center is the school's library. In addition, there is an environmental laboratory, a theater and a therapy room. Three covered patios serve as a break room during bad weather. The whole amoeba-shaped building is surrounded by a "city wall" made of rough exposed masonry.

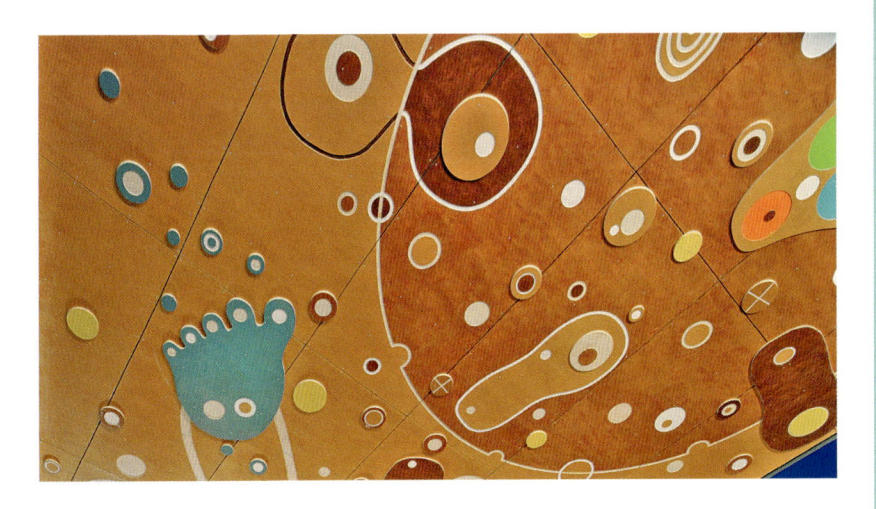

Church of the Good Shepherd
Palosuontie 1
Juha Leiviskä
2003

K 096

Throughout his career Juha Leiviskä has designed many churches, but the Church of the Good Shepherd was a special case: he had to incorporate an existing church, built in 1950 by Yrjö Vaskinen, into his new building. In the meantime a highway was built between the church and the neighborhood. In 1973 the church was extended to accommodate a vestry, parish offices and meeting rooms. In the late Eighties, an architectural design competition for a second extension was awarded to Leiviskä, but initially deferred. On the cramped site the new building goes right up to the property lines. It faces away from the barrier wall that was built to block the noisy street. Leiviskä demolished the altar and bell tower of the existing church and turned the old building into the community hall. At the site of the old altar, old and new meet. A new crypt, a children's playroom and a group space were provided under the new church, accessible via a new staircase. A long porch leads to the main entrance, which is also marked by the bell tower from the road. The new altar wall was carefully planned and composed of wall segments. Four large vertical windows allow natural light in, reflected through prisms, designed by Markku Pääkkönen. The backs of the walls are designed in different colors that bring a slight shimmer into the church. The old altar, representing the Good Shepherd, could not be moved, but a cast was integrated into the new building. The building offers space for 350 worshipers and the community hall holds 550 people. The new church also contains a children's chapel, game rooms, seminar rooms, a music room and church records office.

1952

Olympic Stadium A 097
Paavo Nurmen tie 1
Yrjö Lindegren, Toivo Jäntti
1938

Finnish-Russian School ⩽ K 098
Kaarelankuja 2
Osmo Sipari
1965

The gleaming white Olympic Stadium in the Töölö District is the largest sports stadium in Finland and considered a high point of functionalist architectural design in the country. Many competitions at the 1952 Summer Olympic Games were held here. However, it was originally built for the 1940 Summer Games, which were awarded to Tokyo, and were eventually canceled completely because of the World War II. In 1983 and again in 2005 the World Athletics Championships took place in the Olympic Stadium. During 1990 and 1994 the building was fully refurbished. The 72 meters tall stadium tower is a landmark in the city. The eastern roof over the spectator seats was designed by the architects Kimmo Lintula, Niko Sirola and Mikko Summanen in 2005. Integrated into the Olympic Stadium is the Finnish Sports Museum.

Like most schools in Finland from the Sixties the Finnish-Russian School is made of exposed concrete elements, with two floors and a flat roof. The band window strengthens the horizontal expression. Architect Osmo Sipari developed a pavilion-style layout for the Russian school with each function is housed in a separate building: kindergarten, primary school, secondary school and a dormitory with separate apartments for the teachers and janitors. The building's form three sheltered courtyards allow the guards an excellent overview. The cross-wing contains a cafeteria, library and administrative offices. Auditorium and gymnasium are located in separate buildings. In section, the school is split level to accommodate entrances at different levels depending on the surrounding terrain.

Sports Museum
Paavo Nurmen tie 1
Yrjö Lindegren, Toivo Jäntti
1938

A | 099

Hartwall Arena
Areenankuja 1
AMFI Architects
1997

L | 100

The Sports Museum was founded in the early Thirties and originally known for its impressive collection of skis. During the construction of the Olympic Stadium, a separate new building was planned for the museum. It was supposed to be opened in a west wing in 1938, but when the decision was made that Finland's capital should host the Olympic Games in 1940, the rooms were used for the National Olympic Committee (NOC). Because of the World War II the Helsinki Games were eventually canceled, and in 1943 the rooms were used for the museum as originally planned. Toivo Jäntti also designed the first extension to the museum in 1963.

The stadium was completed in time for the Ice Hockey World Championship in 1997. Ten years later the arena was the venue for the Euro Vision Song Contest, a separate press center having been built as an addition for the occasion. The hall is elliptical, 133 meters long, 103 meters wide and 32 meters high and can be converted for other events. For athletics the capacity is about 10,000 and for concerts 12,000. The hall is also used for conventions. Attached to the Hartwall Arena a multi-story car park which provides space for 1,391 vehicles. An elevator goes below ground, where there is a training rink built into the rock. Behind is a cordoned-off area for gymnastics.

Sonera Stadium
Urheilukatu 1
Ritva Kokkola-Lemarchand et al.
2000

A 101

The Sonera soccer stadium can accommodate 10,700 spectators. It is a seat-only stadium and all seats are covered. The main grandstand can be heated. Games are played on artificial turf and under the playing field there is turf heating. In the stadium the soccer club HJK Helsinki plays its home games, and matches of the Finnish national team are also held here. The 200 meters long, dynamically curved steel structure of the grandstand roof is supposed to "express the power and beauty of movement". The design by Ritva Kokkola-Lemarchand and Olivier Lemarchand won an international architectural design competition. The aim of the designers was "to create a comfortable, safe and attractive environment for players and spectators". The majority of the seats and ancillary rooms are concentrated in the western wing, generating an "urban" side towards the neighborhood. The other three sides of the playing field have only light, non-heated grandstands and 16 kiosks. The substructure consists mainly of precast concrete and the lower rows are of steel. The main structure, a space frame with a triangular cross section, is called a "banana beam". The consoles on which the roof rests are higher than the support and they are fastened with tension cables to the concrete frame of the building's facade. The "banana beam" rests on V-shaped supports. It was produced locally in segments and bolted, each component weighing up to 21 tons. The round roof follows a wave form and it never obstructs the view towards the playing field.

H

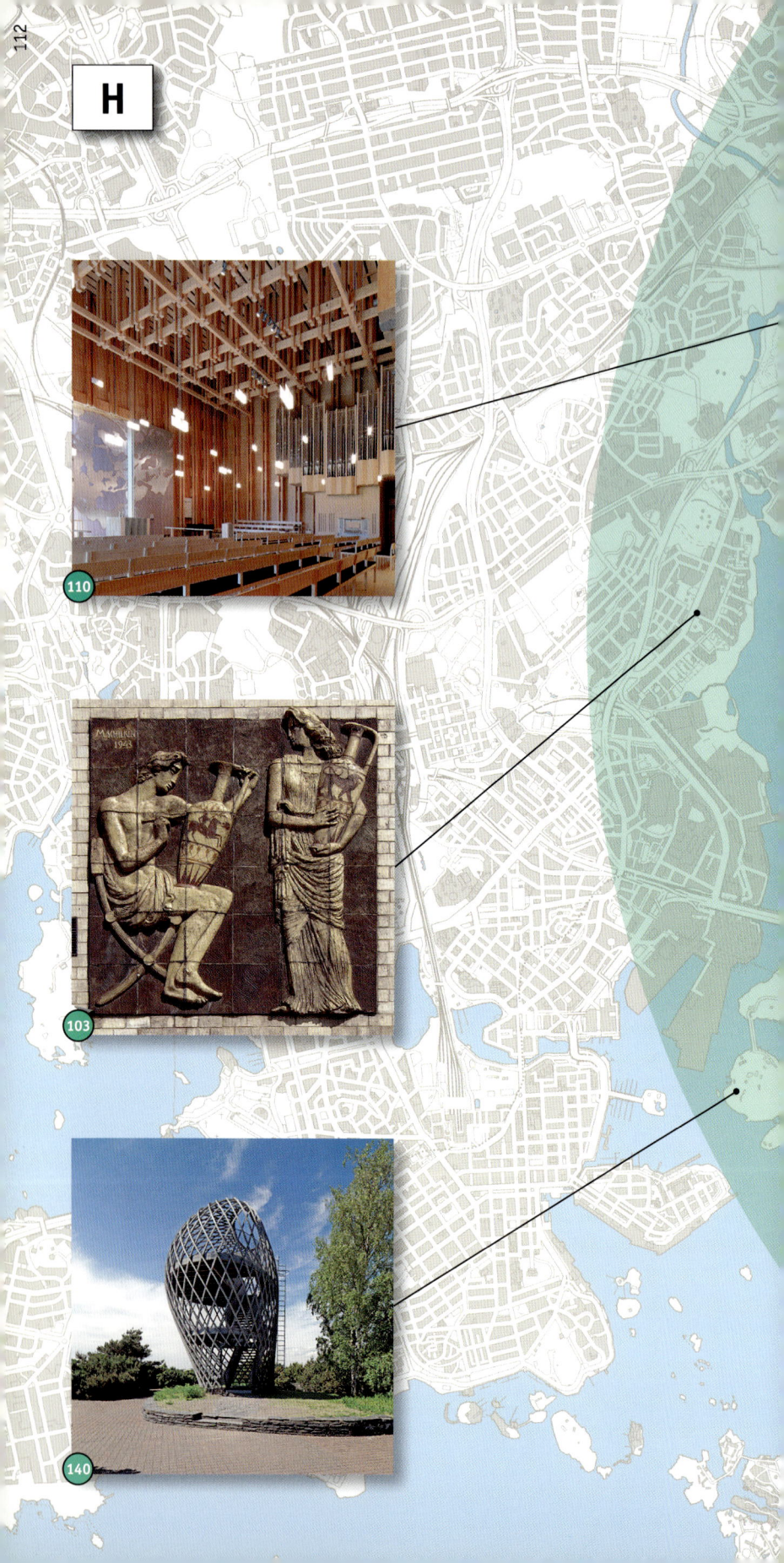

110

103

140

East

House of Culture ⌄ C 102
Sturenkatu 4
Alvar Aalto
1958

Arabia Center L 103
Hämeentie 135a
Karl Malmström et al.
1942

The House of Culture is considered the masterpiece of Alvar Aalto's brick-period. For the curved walls of the auditorium red-brown bricks were custom produced. The community center consists of two parts: an asymmetric, fan-shaped auditorium in the west and a rectangular bar-shaped building with five floors and copper facades in the east. A two-story hall connects the two parts. The auditorium is used for concerts and conferences and can be viewed as a precursor of Aalto's Finlandia Hall. The three components form an open courtyard towards the street. An accompanying pergola frames the square. The concert hall has 1,500 seats.

"Arabia" is the name of the most famous porcelain factory in Finland (it still manufactures ceramics and stoneware) and it's also the name of the district in which the factory stands. The company was founded in 1874 as an offshoot of the Swedish company Rörstrand and the factory building in Helsinki was completed in 1875. In 1884 Arabia became an independent company and since 1916 it has been Finnish-owned. For a long time it was the property of Wärtsilä Yhtymä, but today it is part of the Iittala Group. Parts of the former factory building now house the University of Art and Design. Shops and offices are also included on the site.

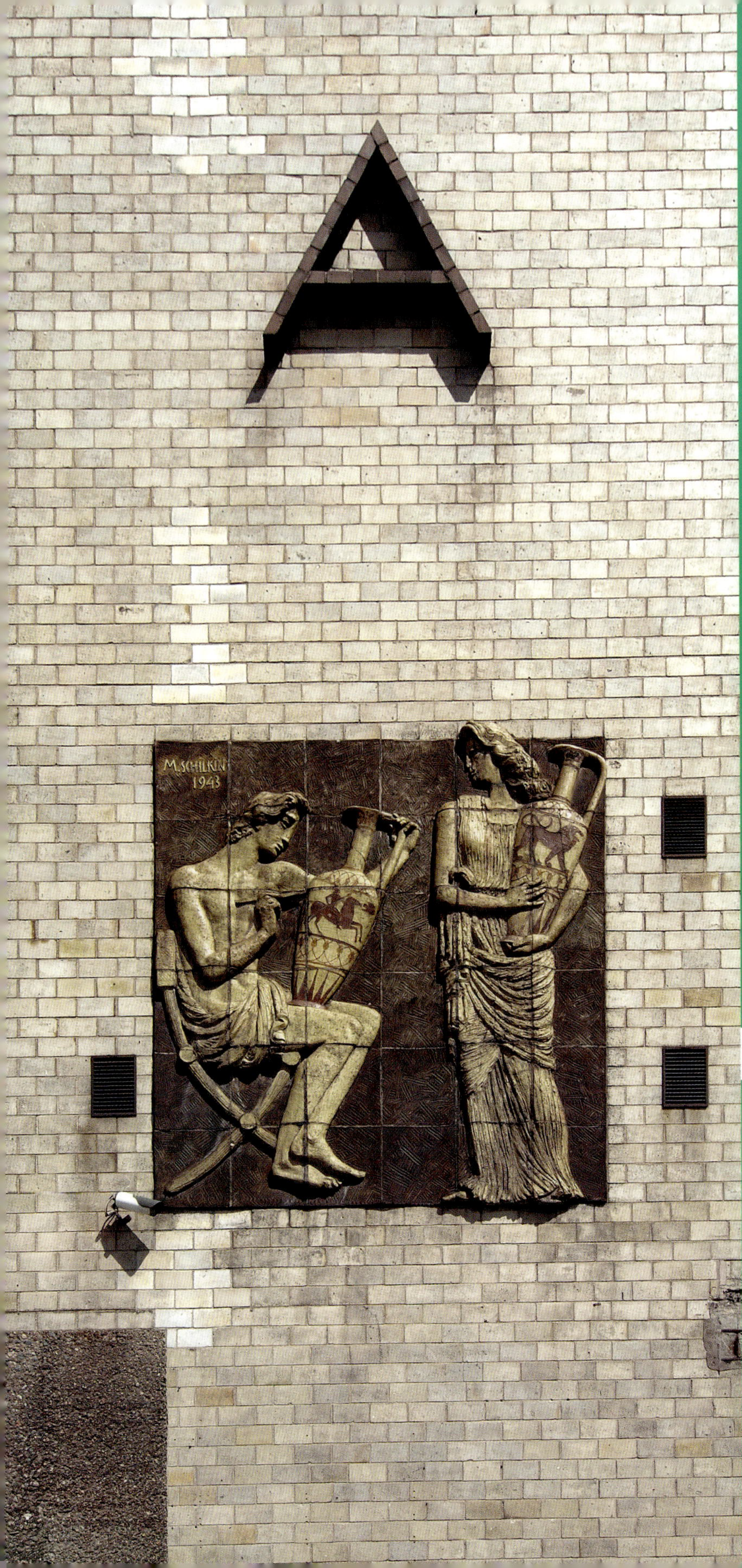
M.SCHILKIN
1943

Pasila Station ≈ 　　　L 104
Ratapihantie 6
CJN Architects
1989

Velodrome ≈ 　　　L 105
Mäkelänkatu 70
Hilding Ekelund
1946

Pasila Station with its ten platforms is located three kilometers north of the main railway station and it's the second most important station in the country. The huge railway yards criss-cross and defines the Pasila District. A station was first established at the site in 1862. Around the station, a cluster of skyscrapers will soon be built and there are plans to make Pasila the new main railway station of Helsinki.

The Velodrome with its 400 meters track was built in preparation for hosting the Helsinki's Summer Olympic Games in 1946 after a design by Hilding Ekelund. In addition to the cycling competitions it was also used for field hockey games, which were held on the grass in the center of the circular course. The glistening white, classical-modern building is listed and was extensively renovated between 1997 and 2000.

Malmi Airport Terminal ⌃ M 106
Tattariharjuntie
Dag Englund, Vera Rosendahl
1938

Embassy of Iraq ⌄ N 107
Lars Sonckin tie 2
Dinkha Latchin Associates
1980

Until the opening of the new airport in Vantaa in 1952, it was the largest airport in the country; in the Thirties all major cities in the country could be reached from Malmi by air. It now serves only commercial flights. Measured by the number of takeoffs and landings, it is still the second most important airport in Finland. The terminal building is circular in plan and includes the air traffic control tower. At right angles to each other two office wings reach away from the circular center and thus frame the drive-up. Circumferential ribbon windows accentuate the horizontality of the building. The first floor contains a restaurant; offices are on the floor above.

Built in 1980 on Vuosaari Island, the Embassy of Iraq looks like a glistening white Arabian palace a long way from home. The single-story Embassy is based on a modular grid made of prefabricated white concrete elements in the shape of mushroom columns. The dark mirror-glass facade is set back from the periphery. The shape of the structure is reminiscent of the Al Kadhimain Mosque in Baghdad. It is adorned with an Arabesque patterning. The Embassy was designed by an Iraqi architect and bears witness to a time when Iraq enjoyed considerable oil-related wealth. Diplomatic relations between Finland and Iraq had already been openend in 1959.

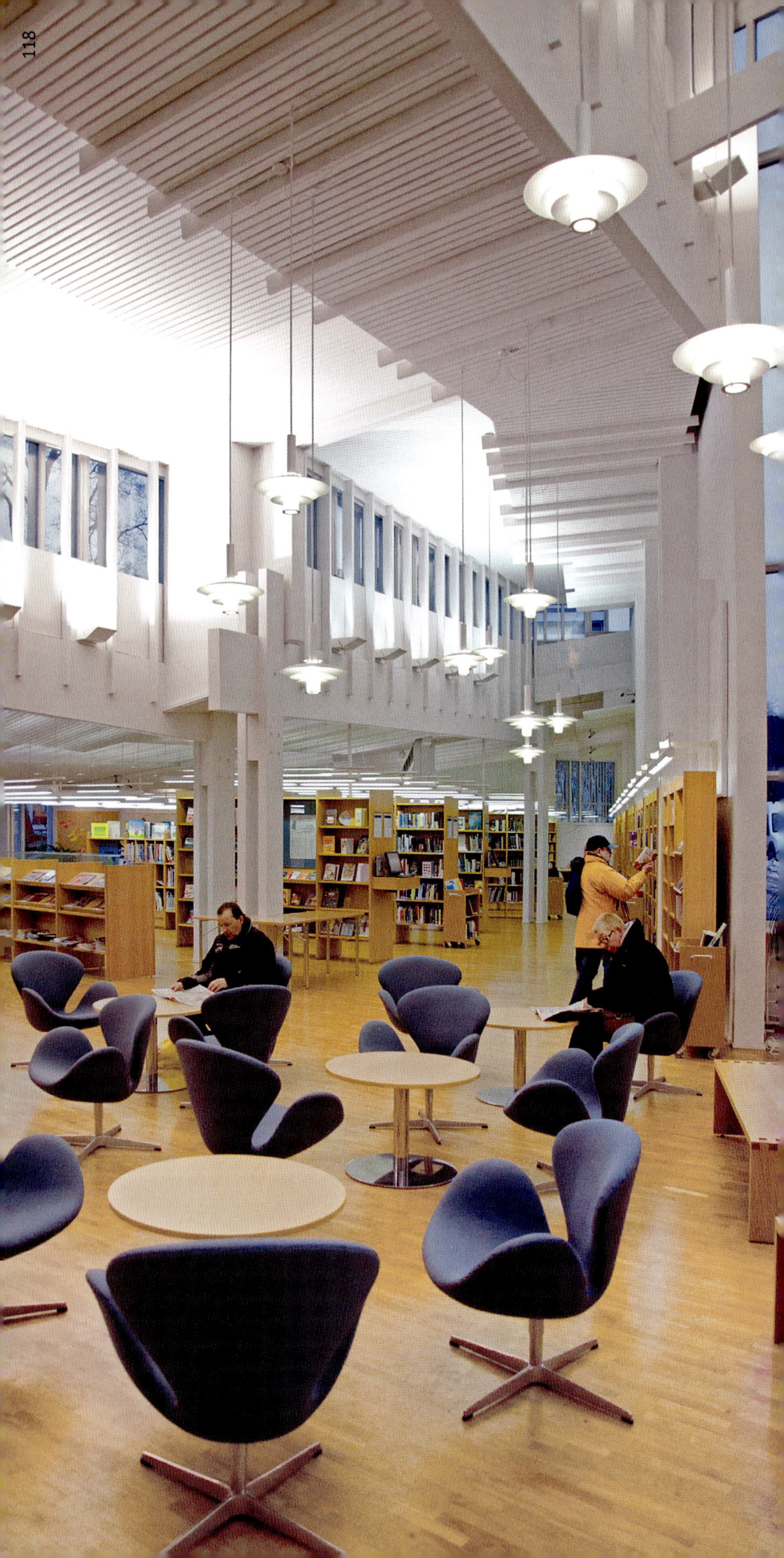

Vallila Library　　　　　　　L 108
Päijänteentie 3-5
Juha Leiviskä, Asta Björklund
1991

Physicum ⌄　　　　　　　　L 109
Vaino Auerin Katu 11
Lahdelma & Mahlamäki
2001

The building forms and materials of the combined library and kindergarten in Vallila reference to the wooden houses in the neighborhood. From the street the library appears fairly closed with white wooden panel facades. Library and kindergarten encircle a central plaza. Although the library only has one story, it has different ceiling heights and different intensities of daylight from above. The bookshelves are low in the middle and high at the perimeter. The laminated wooden columns and trusses are left exposed. The 920 square meters tall library has oak parquet floors, which give the central hall, furnished with comfortable armchairs, a cozy character.

For the construction of the Physicum of the University of Helsinki an architectural competition was held in 1997 from which Lahdelma & Mahlamäki emerged the winners. The new building on the Kumpula campus is part of a long term plan to relocate the labs, teaching and research facilities of several departments away from the city and consolidate them on three new sites. The building stands on Kumpula Hill, one of the highest points in Helsinki. It serves the physics department and houses a library for the entire campus. The facades are of white concrete and untreated aluminum, which can also be found inside. Wooden surfaces inside create a warm atmosphere.

120

Viikki Church
Agronominkatu 5
JKMM Architects
2005

M 110

While in other European countries churches are closing down and mostly mosques are the only sacred buildings to be built from scratch, Christian church architecture in Finland is not yet dead. There are new wooden churches in the suburbs of Helsinki, showing how deeply rooted the original Protestant concept of space is in Northern Europe. While the bright rooms made of wood may not be comparable to the dark mysticism of Baroque churches, nevertheless these have a special symbolism: Wood is a natural, renewable resource that creates a warm and almost friendly atmosphere inside the building. In the Latokartano neighborhood the Viikki Church stands out because of its facades made of untreated gray aspen wood shingles which, over time acquire a silver patina. Tightly packed wooden pillars dominate its entire space. The supporting structure of the 1,600 square meters tall building is made of glue-laminated timber, which has already been prefabricated in sections. The skeleton is reinforced with concrete walls. The walls' lattice-clad laminated veneer wood panels act as part of the supporting structure. Horizontal boards shape the community rooms and vertical squares of bright, radially sawn spruce timber the bell tower. For the ceiling molded veneer elements have been used. The wooden surfaces of the halls were washed with brine. The design by JKMM Architects won first prize in an architectural design competition in 2000 and the church was completed five years later.

St. Matthew's Church »
Turunlinnantie 1–3
Björn Krogius et al.
1984

N 111

Björn Krogius and Veli-Pekka Tuominen won the architectural competition in 1977. St. Matthew's Church is located in a cultural center near the Itäkeskus Shopping Center, called "Stoa". On one side of a square stands the St. Matthew's Church and on the other the community center with two theaters, a two-story library, a youth center and the Stoa café. The blue sculpture in the center of the square was designed by Hannu Sirén.

Vuosaari Church ⌃ ↗
Satamasaarentie 7
Pirkko and Arvi Ilonen
1980

N 112

Mellunkylä Church ⌄
Emännänpolku 1
Käpy and Simo Paavilainen
1988

M 113

Vuosaari Church consists of two components: the prayer room and a community area with several apartments. An internal passage connects the two parts and the main entrance. The roof of the church itself rises from this low passage to a high point. The altar is made of concrete and was designed by Mauri Favén. The church seats 300 people. Vuosaari Church was extended and renovated by the same architects in 2006.

The elongated church is located on a hillside. The bell tower marks the atrium and a large glass front entrance entices visitors into the church. The red brick facade with horizontal stripes shapes the exterior and the interior of the 3,300 square meters tall building. The chapel accomodates 300 worshipers and the smaller community hall 250. The rooms can be connected with each other. Skylights allow daylight to penetrate the church.

Laajasalo Church ⌄
Reposalmentie 13
Kari Järvinen, Merja Nieminen
2003

N 114

The main rooms of the Laajasalo Church lie on a street corner and open up towards a small park at the rear. The bell tower marks the entrance to the community wing along the road. From the lower foyer the path proceeds to a higher pergola hall and finally into the brightly lit chapel. Several light towers illuminate the garden at night from the inside and bring daylight into the room. The structure and the facades of the Laajasalo Church are made entirely of wood. The walls are made of laminated timber panels and columns and the ceilings of laminated wooden beams with steel connections. The bracing concrete walls and steel elements emphasize the contrast with the warm wood. The facade of the great hall is copper-clad with horizontal bands, the inner walls are made of rough-sawn pine, however, and birch which is lacquered or untreated. The floors are made of oiled pine. The facades made of pine planks were painted ocher. Daylight falls onto the altar wall in such a way that it is possible to tell the time of day from the light and shadow.

Korona Info Center ⌃
Viikkinkaari 11a
ARK-house Architects
1999

M 115

Environmental Center ⌐
Viikkinkaari 2a
Kimmo Kuismanen
2011

M 116

The Korona Info Center in the new district of Viikki is a round solitaire in the center of the University of Helsinki Viikki Campus and carved out of the rock on one side. A quarter of the circular floor plan serves as a courtyard. The building has a striking blue front, and the glass sections are designed as double facades. Three gardens or "parks" as they may be called the – "Nile Arboretum", the "Roman Garden" and the "Kyoto Bamboo Garden" – are located between the facade and the rooms. The building houses the large Science Library and the departmental libraries of the Faculty of Agriculture and Forestry as well as lecture and conference halls. The high, canyon-like hallways are partly lit by skylights, the auditorium is covered with plywood and a cafeteria with a beautiful terrace is oriented towards the plaza. Ark-house Architects' (Markku Erholtz, Hannu Huttunen and Pentti Kareoja) winning competition entry has created a remarkable sustainable building, its triple glazed envelope outside a concrete wall providing an in-between space that acts as a climatic buffer, heating incoming air.

The Environmental Center of the City and the University of Helsinki is housed in a building in Viikki that was designed as a model for energy-saving architecture. The building's south facades are covered with photovoltaic panels that also serve as shading elements. The ground floor houses an exhibition on environmentally friendly building techniques and the new Viikki area in general. The building boasts the lowest energy consumption in Finland – less than half that of a normal building of the same size. To cool the Environmental Center in summer geothermal cooling is used from the bedrock below. Other features are the use of district heating, detailed energy monitoring, good windows and tight and well insulated walls. There are additional solar panels and four wind turbines on the roof. Only LED lights are used and occupancy sensors turn off the lights when no one is in the room. The ventilation is zone-specific and there is heat recovery system. On top of that the building has water-saving faucets, energy-efficient office equipment and sheltered bicycle parking.

Stakes Office Building ⌄
Lintulahdenkuja 4
Mikko Heikkinen et al.
2002

C 117

This double office building by Mikko Heikkinen, Marku Komonen and Janne Kentala serves the Stakes organization and the Senate Properties Office. It consists of a renovated former vegetable and grain warehouse and a new building. The users are the state real estate office and the National Research Institute for Welfare and Health, called "Stakes". The red brick facade combines the old and new buildings visually. The former warehouse is dominated by concrete silos and mushroom-shaped pillars. The courtyard facades were opened up and the narrow windows have been widened. The new wing has transparent facades with windows arranged in pairs and with brise-soleil elements. In the former silos only functional elements were accommodated, which do not require daylight, such as stairs and elevators. A railway tunnel that cuts through the building has been preserved and now serves as an entrance marked by five steel columns. The height of the new building matches that of the older one and the top floors are set back. On the roof, the boxes concealing the ventilation systems are covered with copper and a terrace with sea views is planted with vines and trees, its floor is covered with broken bricks. In the courtyard there is a grid of lights and trees grow in steel planters.

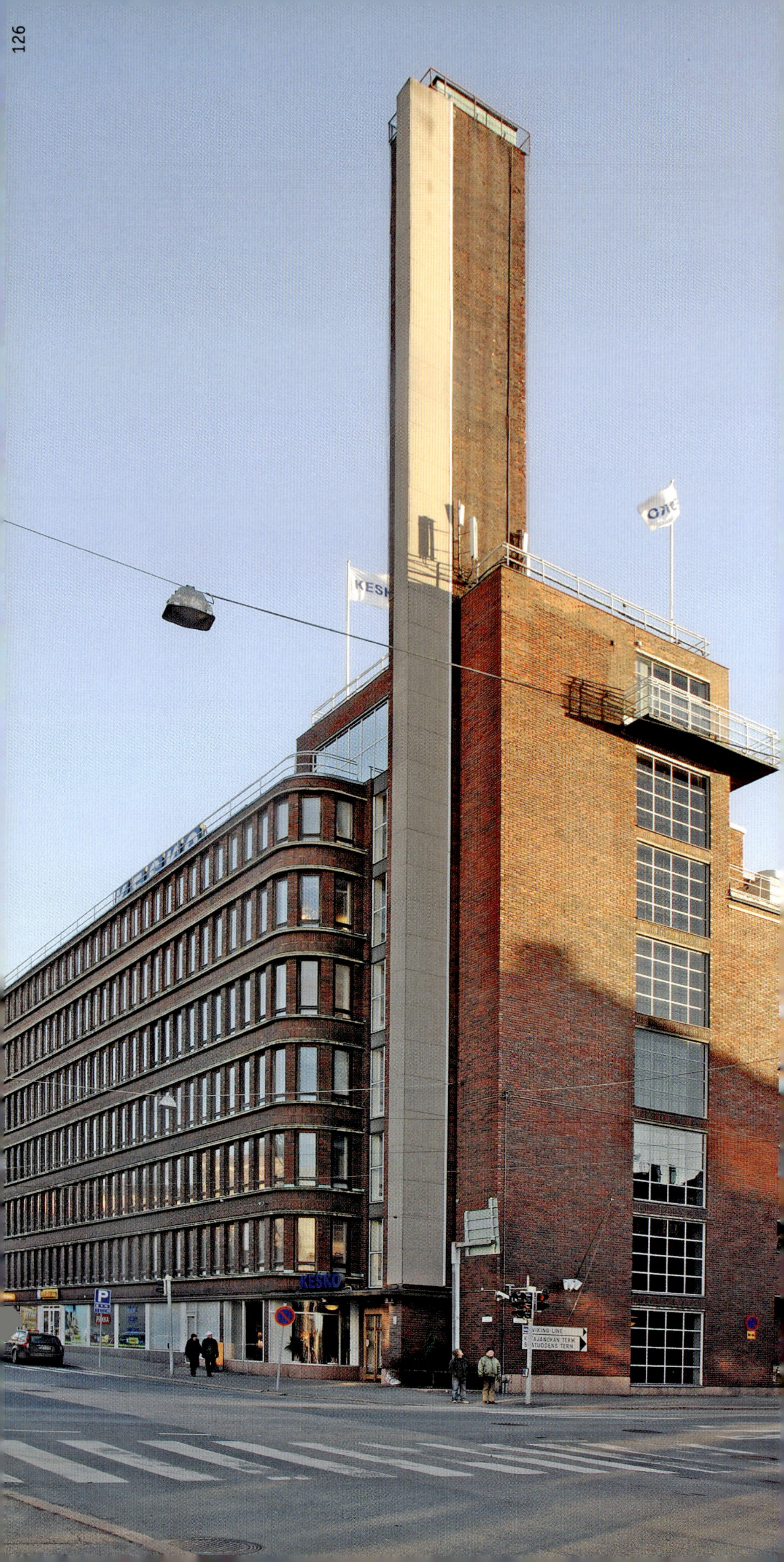

Elanto Headquarters ⌃
Kaikukatu 2
Väinö Vähäkallio
1928

C 118

Eka Warehouse ⌄
Lintulahdenkatu 10
Väinö Vähäkallio
1927

C 119

The grounds of the Elanto Cooperative are home to warehouses, production facilities and the head office. The headquarters building has a tall tower towards Hämeentie. Bay windows divide its red brick facades and the entrance is accented with granite. On the ground floor there were originally several shops. The office floors are double-loaded. The top floor has an auditorium, a cafeteria and a library, the interiors were designed by Birger Hahl. A year after its completion a little extension along Kaikukatu was inaugurated and extended again in 1942.

This central warehouse of the Eka cooperative is a ten-story, monumental brick building. An arcade with rounded arches on one side was originally used as the loading dock, the facade above is divided into long vertical bays. The top floors are set back. The vertical layout makes reference to the adjacent Elanto Warehouse, which was also designed by architect Väinö Vähäkallio and built almost simultaneously. The structure is based on mushroom-shaped concrete columns. In 1992, the storehouse was converted into an office building by Juhani Katainen.

KESKO Headquarters «
Satamakatu 3
Toivo Paatela
1940

D 120

A tall tower marks the entrance to the headquarters of the KESKO cooperative trade organization. The facades made of red brick on three sides lead around the building block. Along the Kanavakatu there are storage rooms behind the band facade and along the Satamakatu are offices behind a perforated facade. Behind the third facade there used to be a coffee roasting-facility.

Arena Building ⌃   C 121
Hämeentie 2
Lars Sonck
1923

Eka Headquarters ⌄   C 122
Hämeentie 19
Väinö Vähäkallio
1933

In 1916 – when the street railway company opened Helsinki's east – the owner of the land Waldemar Aspelin, sold block 301 to the Arena company. The Arena Building, designed by Lars Sonck, stands on a triangular plot of land and was erected in two phases between 1924 and 1929 as a commercial and residential premises near Hakaniemi Square. The triangular building of red brick frames the square's north side. All stairwells and service rooms are oriented towards the inner courtyard, so that all three street facades can have uniformly perforated walls. In an unusual feature the Arena Building is surrounded by tram tracks on all sides. In 2010 the building was extensively renovated, the windows restored and the courtyard faithfully preserved. The "Arena Tower" contained the first radio station in Finland in 1924. In the past, there were also two cinemas in the building. The Northwest Tower was originally a laundry room. Having stood empty for many years, the tower has now been converted into an offices building. Between 1995 and 2010 a cabaret theater occupied the ground floor.

The distinguishing corner building at Hämeentie serves as the headquarters of the Eka cooperative. A nine-story tower, circular in plan, emphasizes the street corner. The building's main entrance is located at the intersection of the tower with the roadside, six-story office wing. A real estate firm bought the building, designed by Väinö Vähäkallio, in 2006 and presently leases the 22,000 square meters of office space.

Malmi Church ⌃
Kunnantie 1
Kristian Gullichsen
1980

M 123

Ympyrätalo Building ⌄
Siltasaarenkatu 18
Kaija and Heikki Siren
1965

C 124

Malmi Church has largely closed off red brick facades towards the street. Its hidden entrance is reached via a small courtyard in the rear, which frames the building. Worshipers enter via the long side. The altar wall gets daylight through a light from above through a light slit. The baptismal font is expressed with a semicircular niche. On the opposite side of the vestibule there is two-story community hall. The social rooms are upstairs.

The "Ympyrätalo" (circular building) is a commercial building with a circular floor plan. Previously there were a number of wooden buildings and the stone house "Wendt" on the site. Users of the building enjoy a view of the Hakaniemi Plaza on one side and of the Hesperia Park on the other. Since 2000 the building with more than 35,000 square meters space has been owned by the Ilmarinen Pension Insurance. It was renovated in 2004.

Itäkeskus Shopping Center
Itäkatu 1-7
Erkki Kairamo, Heikki Mäkinen
1984

N 125

The Itäkeskus District is home to the largest fully enclosed shopping center in Northern Europe. It offers more than 120,000 square meters of retail space, contains 300 shops and 30 restaurants and follows an American suburban pattern. It consists of four parts called, "Pasaasi", "Pikku-Bulevardi", "Bulevardi" and "Piazza". The bottom two of the five floors contain shops with garage parking and office space above. The "Pasaasi" was opened in 1984 and has direct access to a nearby subway station. Another 160 stores were added in 1992, in the large and small "Bulevardi". The "Piazza" followed in 2001 and later the "Prism" (extensions by Juhani Pallasmaa, Mikko Heikkinen and Marko Komonen, Pekka Helin and Tuomo Siitonen in 1992, Jukka Karhunen and Seppo Juha Ilonen Häkli in 2001 and 2006).

Helsinki Seafarers' Center ⌃
Provianttikatu 4
ARK-house Architects
2009

M 126

Iiris Center for the Blind ⌄
Marjaniementie 74
Rainer Mahlamäki
2005

N 127

The Helsinki Seafarers' Center was built in the new Vuosaari port of Helsinki for the Finnish seafaring mission. The building stands at the northern end at the entrance to the port, so it's easily visible to people on incoming ships. The Seafarer's Center is the only building that references to natural forms in the new hi-tech port. It has organic, soft shapes and a wooden facade. It blends into the small hill with trees and rocks at the rear. The gently curved walls evoke the world of ships, while the plan is reminiscent of a fish. The Helsinki Seafarers' Center offers mariners a first port of call. On its 320 square meters of space it contains a café, laundry facilities, computer workstations and a small sauna. The building has also been dedicated as a church – worship, weddings and baptisms can all take place here.

The Iiris Building is a service and cultural center for the blind and visually impaired. It was designed specifically to meet the needs of the visually impaired and deaf-blind and also serves as a training and conference center. During the day rehabilitation and vocational training courses take place here and during the evening and at weekends there are cultural and social activities. The clear rectangular floor plan facilitates orientation. All signs and labels are large and also executed in Braille with other tactile or acoustic signals. The auditorium has 100 seats and special acoustic technology has been installed for the deaf-blind. In addition ther are meeting rooms and a Braille library. Strong contrasts and colors and wheelchair access doors that open through light barriers, make this a model for a disabled-friendly building.

EN NÄYTTÄMÖN
ATESÄILYTYS

Municipal Theater
Eläintarhantie 5
Timo Penttilä
1976, 1989

C 128

Hanasaari B Power Plant ⩹
Parrukatu 1
Timo Penttilä et al.
1974, 1976

C 129

The Helsinki City Theater is located on a hillside in a park and it consists of long horizontal components, granite walls and a roof that extend far out into the surroundings. The large, glass-enclosed lobby of the theater offers glimpses into the park and Eläintarhanlahti. The building has a large and a small hall. The floor plan of the large hall with 920 seats represents a traditional proscenium theater, but the small stage with 300 seats can be used flexibly. The facade is covered with bright ceramic tiles. As with Alvar Aalto's Finlandia Hall, the fly tower serves as the only vertical element. The design by Timo Penttilä reconciles modernity with the landscape.

The Hansaari B coal-fired power plant produces electricity and heat for the inner city. It was designed by Timo Penttilä, Jouni Ijäs and Heikki Saarela. Its predecessor, called "A", was demolished. All additional functions such as offices and staircases are grouped around the large central power plant hall creating a diverse structure, which is held together visually by the uniform design of the facades. In the future the coal-bearing structure will be housed more discretely in a silo, because the neighborhood has been reclassified as a residential area. Currently, an additional power plant is being built for peak loads. The coal is delivered by ship.

SOK Factory ⌃　　　　　　L 130
Sturenkatu 17
Erkki Huttunen
1938

Malmi Post Office ⌄　　　131
Hietakummuntie 19
Matti Nurmela et al.
1986

Erkki Huttunen, the architect for the non-profit trade group SOK, created series of well-designed commercial buildings in a functional way. The SOK Factory, in which roasted coffee and spices are stored, was completed in 1938. It has a white plastered wall and the facade is characterized by long, narrow ribbon windows that give the building a horizontal emphasis. The windows of the factory go around the corner.

Designed by Matti Nurmela, Kari Raimoranta and Jyrki Tasa, the post office in the suburb of Malmi fronts the local square with an unusually tall, table-like canopy above the main entrance. A glass cylinder connects the Post Office's different floors adjacent to the main hall. The building also houses a cafeteria, a health center and a caretaker's apartment. The plaster walls have colored strips of ceramic tiles.

Sörnäinen Office Building ≈ C 132
Sörnäisten rantatie 23
Kaarina Löfström et al.
1988

Pasila Library ≈ L 133
Rautatieläisenkatu 8
Kaarlo Leppänen
1986

This office building by Kaarina Löfström, Matti Mäkinen and Mauri Tommila with its rounded corner stands on a triangular site. Like the warehouses in the neighborhood it also has a band facade, but not in red brick, but clad with green ceramic tiles. Left and right of the corner tower, which acts as a hinge, there are cellular offices along a double corridor. The corner tower contains a cafeteria and conference rooms.

The main Library of the City of Helsinki is located in the district of East Pasila. It was built in 1986 by Kaarlo Leppänen and remodeled and extended in 1996. The library has eight kilometers of shelving and it is organized around a naturally lit courtyard with fountains. The neighborhood has sidewalks on two levels and the building thus gives access on both levels. The facades are covered in dark blue ceramic tiles.

136

Itäkeskus Swimming Pool N 134
Olavinlinnantie 6
Jukka Karhunen et al.
1993

Center for Teacher Education ≽ M 135
Kevätkatu 2
Markku Erholtz et al.
2003

The Itäkeskus Swimming Pool was blasted out of the rock and it can be used as a temporary shelter for 3,800 people in an emergency. The raw rock walls are partially sprayed with white concrete and contrast with the colorful architectural details. Because of the absence of daylight the architectural design was even more important. The alternate brief for the civil defense use brought with it strict requirements for air conditioning and lighting. The acoustics needed to be improved with acoustic sails.

At the new teacher-training facility of the University of Helsinki 250 trainee teachers meet more than 900 students of all ages. The design by Markku Erholtz, Hannu Huttunen and Jussi Karjalainen won first prize in an architectural design competition. The building is organized along an internal path with classrooms on either side. The cafeteria, library and large foyer serve as a social center. From the central spine, the human eye is always directed towards the differently designed schoolyards.

LUME Audiovisual Center L 136
Muotoilijankatu 3
ARK-house Architects
2002

Itäkeskus Landmark Tower ⌃ N 137
Kauppakartanonkatu 7
Erkki Kairamo
1987

The LUME Audiovisual Center in Arabianranta is defined by its colorful, abstract facade of corrugated sheet metal. The facade of the building is clad with silvery shimmering sheets and the colorful signature "Lume". The building is used for training, research and development of audio-visual media by the University of Art & Design Helsinki and contains studios, media labs and meeting rooms, film and television studios, a black box theater and an auditorium. A glass passage leads from the main entrance on Hämeentie to the production and performance halls.

This 16-story tower has a square floor plan with all four corners diagonally cut off. As a result the 20 meters wide tower seems particularly slim, its design reminiscent of British hi-tech architecture. The stairwell is glazed and separated from the main tower. The ventilation ducts are deliberately left visible in part to give the facade its technological appearance. They are clad in white and green tiles. The steel components are painted turquoise and gray. The office areas are shaped like a ring around the central elevator core. On the top floor there is a conference room and a sauna.

EVIRA Food Safety Office ≈ ≽   M 138
Mustialankatu 3
Lahdelma & Mahlamäki
2006

Sonera Offices ≽   L 139
Elimäenkatu 5
SARC
2000

The new headquarters of the Finnish Food Safety Authority EVIRA has been built in the Viikki Science Park. It combines the 500 employees from the existing offices in Helsinki and Vantaa. Besides offices, the new building, designed by Lahdelma & Mahlamäki, also contains laboratories. The EVIRA organization is also responsible for the animal and plant protection in Finland.

The design of this office building for the Sonera Telecommunications company fits into its industrial neighborhood. The street facade of the building with its 17,000 square meters of office space is clad in black, printed glass. The double facade is open top and bottom and has a horizontal expression. The main entrance is on the diagonal corner and leads to an atrium with a spiral staircase.

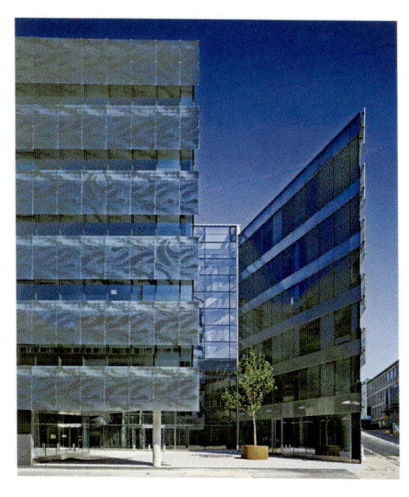

4

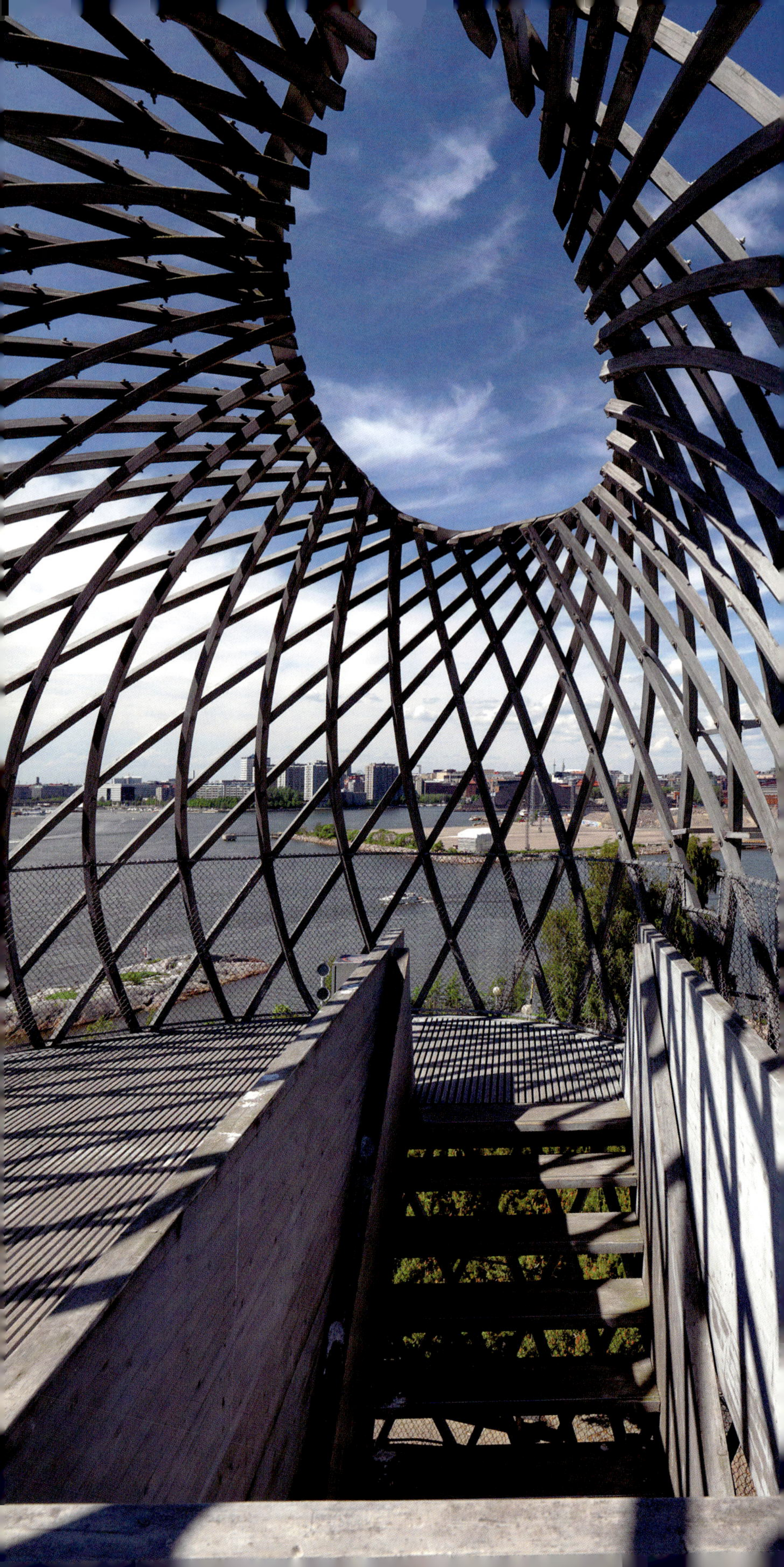

Kupla Observation Tower « C 140
Mustikkamaanpolku 12
Avanto Architects et al.
2002

Roofing for the Zoo C 141
Mustikkamaanpolku 12
Beckmann N'Thépé
2014

At the invitation of the Helsinki Zoo and Wood Focus Finland in 1999 a competition was organized for the students of the University of Helsinki to design a ten meters high observation tower made of wood. The winning design by Ville Hara has a cage-like shell in a free form and is called "Kupla" (bubble). With the help of actual and computer models its form was finalized and simplified. The preformed laminated timber elements were, as is usual in boatbuilding, treated with steam in order to mold them into the desired shapes, then linseed oil was applied to the surfaces. The teardrop shape of the observation deck became a symbol for Korkesaari Island and can easily be seen by the passing large passenger ferries, because it stands 18 meters above sea level. The oval tower has three floors. Like an eggshell the lattice shell can withstand pressure. Eight students built the pavilion.

The Zoo in Helsinki is over 100 years old, but for 30 years no polar bears were on display there. Currently the city wants to redevelop the Zoo. French architects Beckmann-N'Thépé with TN + landscape architects won the competition for the new building. Their proposal foresees a huge structure which creates a new entrance to the Zoo on Korkesaari Island. The large glass dome will incorporate the box office, auditorium, restaurant and souvenir shops, and be the new home for polar bears. The architecture should be subordinate to the landscape, and still be a new landmark. The interiors will be characterized by light, reflections, and depth and are to be reminiscent of a walkable glacial landscape. The surrounding 26-acre park will be divided into four zones: Arctic, Central Asian steppe, Asian forest and Central Asian mountains. They will give the park changing faces depending on the season.

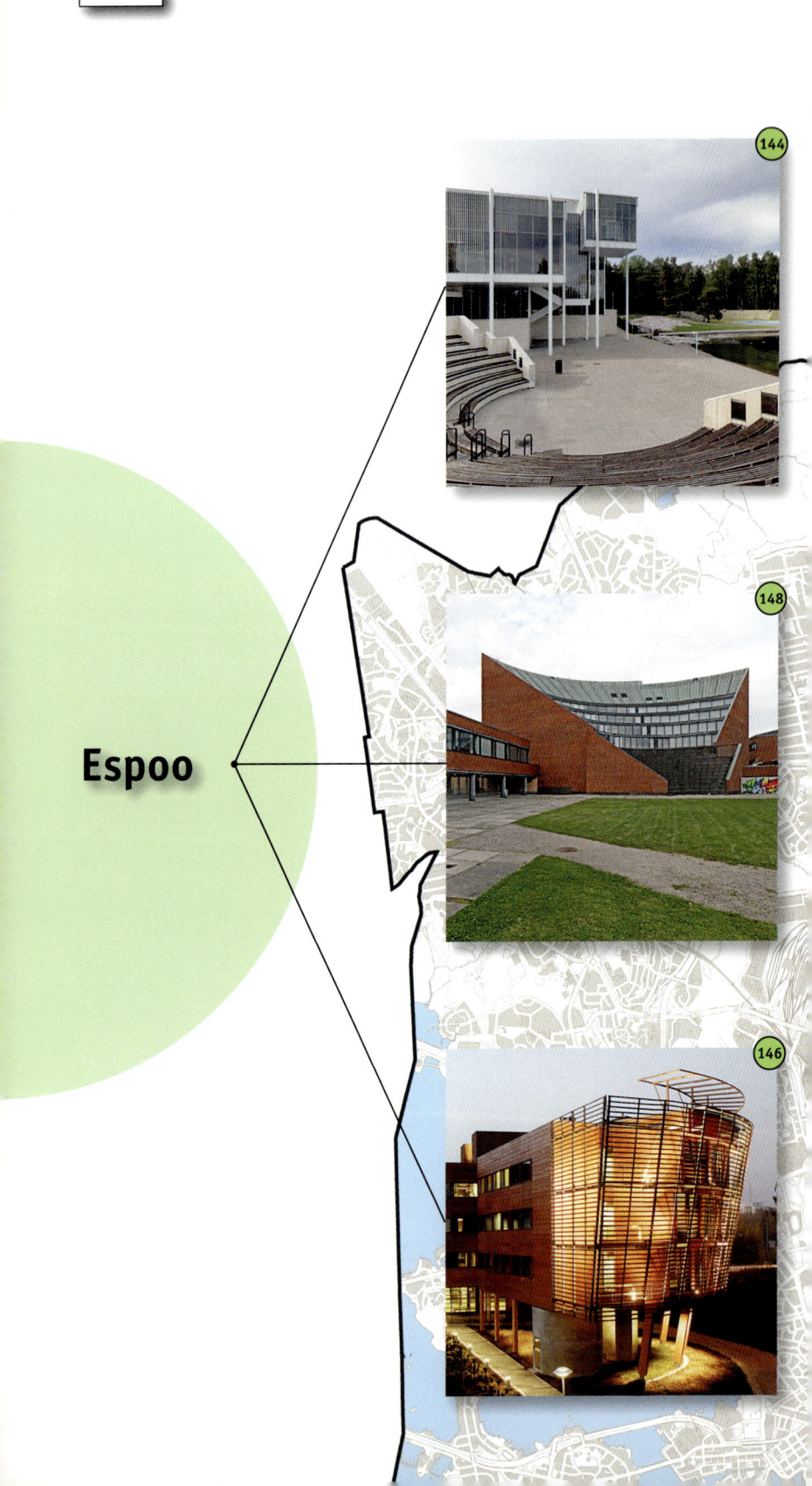

J

Espoo

144

148

146

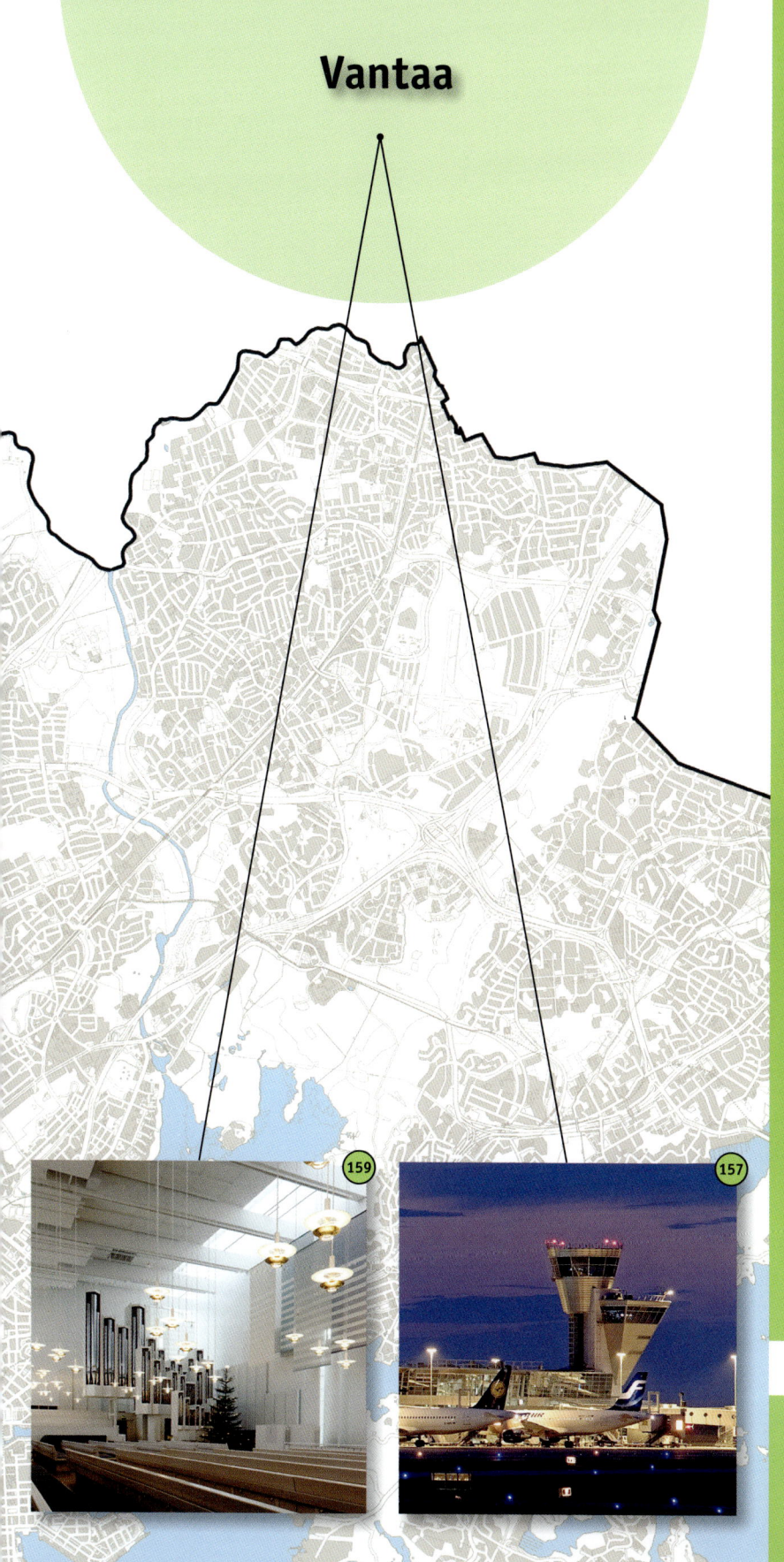

Vantaa

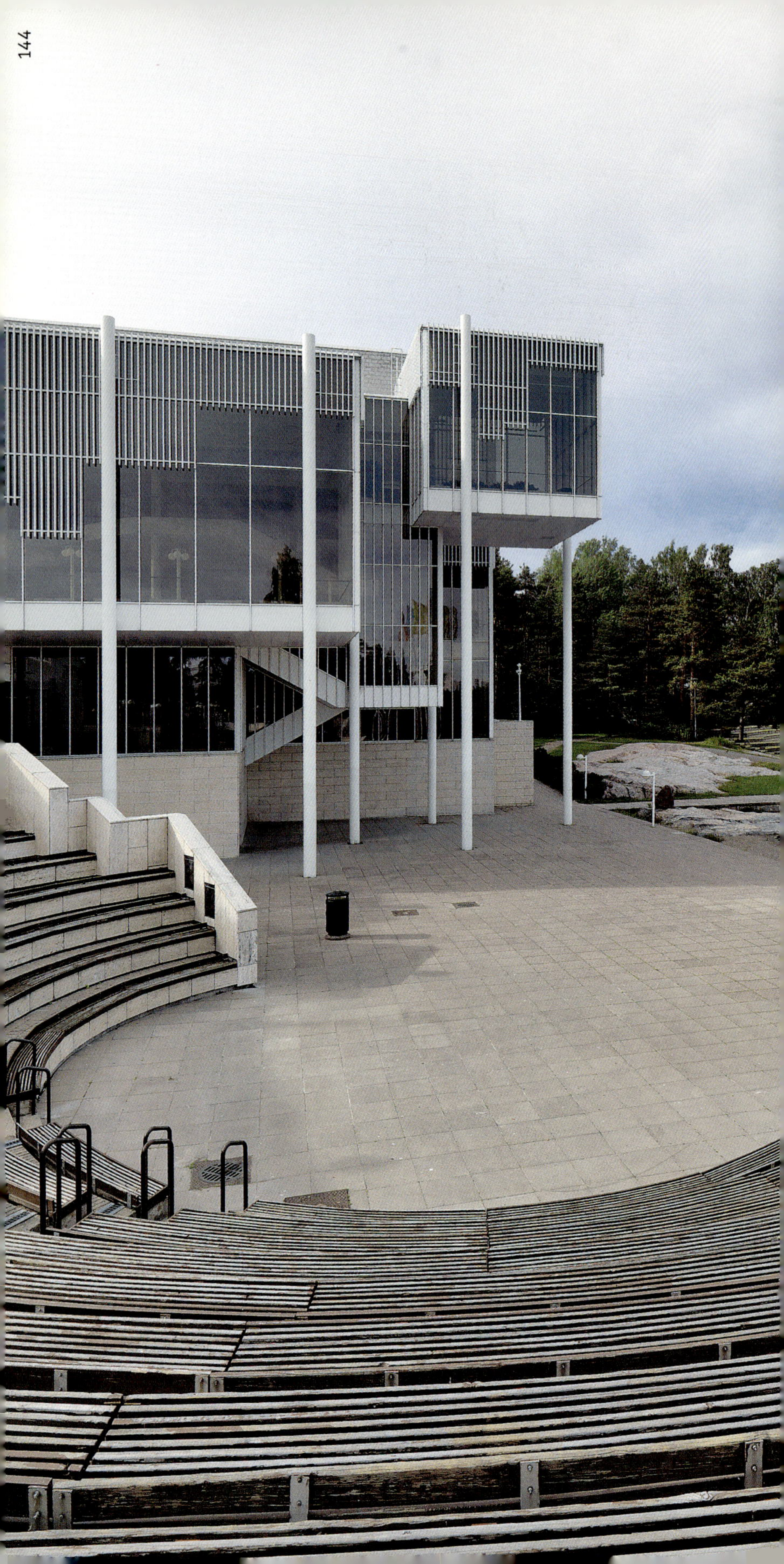

Fortum Headquarters ⌃   L 142
Keilaniementie 1, Espoo
Castrén Jauhiainen Nuuttila
1978

Kone Building ⌃   L 143
Keilasatama 3, Espoo
Antti-Matti Siikala / SARC
2001

The headquarters of the Fortum Corporation is a high-rise tower on the lake. The building was critical in developing Keilaniemi as a major office location: with a height of 84 meters it is the second tallest building in Finland. The current user is the state owned power company Fortum. However, the building was built for the oil company Neste, which subsequently merged with the predecessor of Fortum but eventually split off again. The Neste Oil Corporation then built their own headquarters next door.

The corporate office tower of the elevator manufacturer Kone looks like a simple glass box. The 72 meters high glass facade shows a glass elevator shaft, in which the four traveling lifts are clearly visible. No lift crossing disturbs the abstract silhouette of the building for the Kone company, whose development of the crossing-free elevators became world famous. Only the top six floors are used by Kone; the company's headquarters is still located on the historic Munkkiniemi estate in Helsinki.

Espoo Cultural Center « »   144
Kaupinkalliontie 10, Espoo
Arto Sipinen
1989

The Espoo Cultural Center in the heart of Tapiola has its lobby oriented to the water basin. The Tapiola Sinfonietta, the Espoo City Theater, a jazz and film festival, exhibitions and a piano festival plus a week of choral music fill the center of cultural life in Espoo, Finland's fastest growing city. The building contains an auditorium with 788 seats and a theater with 300 seats, a library, music school, adult education center and an exhibition hall. Arto Sipinen has divided the large space into smaller blocks and orientates them toward the basin. The facades are made of brushed white Roman travertine, yellow brick and glass; those of the great halls are closed and oriented away from the basin. The staccato of small cubes into which the foyer is broken down is reflected in the water's surface. The plaza has an open-air theater and a waterfall. The entrances are located on the forecourt and from the basin. The lounges on two levels overlook the water.

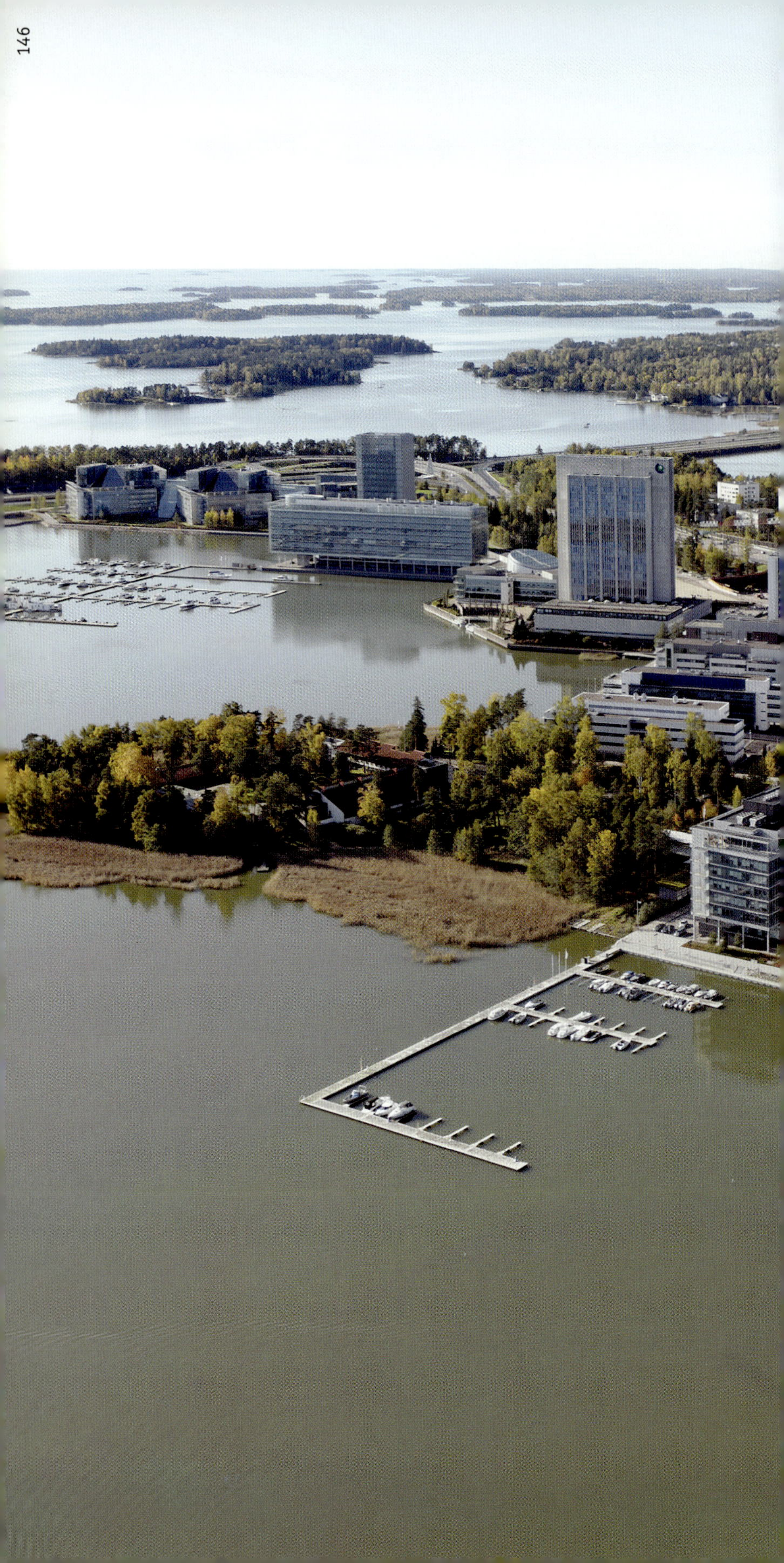

147

5

Tapiola Swimming Pool ⌃
Kirkkopolku 3, Espoo
Aarne Ervi
1968

145

FMO Finnforest Building ⌄
Tuulikuja, Espoo
Pekka Helin
2005

146

On the north side of the central basin in Tapiola lies the indoor swimming pool, designed by Aarne Ervi. Patrons enter the building from the upper level through a gallery. Glass facades and a circular skylight dome shape the design. During athletic competitions, viewers can sit on spectator stands. The complex also has two outdoor pools: a diving pool and a wading pool, around which sun terraces are arranged in an amphitheater-like layout. In 2006 the building was renovated and expanded by Nurmela, Raimoranta, Tasa (NRT) – saunas, jacuzzis and a gym were added.

The FMO (Finnforest Modular Office) Building is a four-story office building that proves that a human and environmentally friendly architecture can be achieved in timber. It consists of three modules with rectangular courtyards. Laminated wood, which comes exclusively from sustainably managed forests, was used for the structure. The facade consists of 1,200 parts which were prefabricated and another 17,000 individually molded wooden elements. All fire safety standards were met. A total of 2,400 cubic meters of wood were used in the FMO Finnforest Building.

WeeGee Building
Ahertajantie 5, Espoo
Aarno Ruusuvuori
1966

The WeeGee Building was originally built as a print works for the Weilin & Göös Corporation. The production process defined the open floor plan, so that the print facilities could be installed as flexibly as possible. The number of columns were therefore kept to a minimum and all partition walls were moveable. The print workshop on the upper floor has only one column per 729 square meters of floor space. The two-story concrete building is based on a square grid of 9 × 9 meters. The round concrete shafts go from the basement up through the roof and incorporate the airconditioning ducts. Roof elements are suspended from eight diagonals. The windows are designed to avoid direct sunlight in the south facade and let indirect daylight into the hall, which is optimal for printing. The northern facade is fully glazed and afford views of the surrounding forest. The first two phases were built in 1964 and 1966. Aarno Ruusuvuori was also supposed to build the third phase of the administration wing, but after a change of ownership in 1974, the engineering firm Bertel Ekengren completed the building. The fourth section was never built because printing ceased on the site. The building was used as a gym for some time before it was rebuilt in 2006 to a design by Timo Airas for Henna Helander, who turned it into Espoo's art center containing five museums.

Technical University ⌃
Otakaari 1, Espoo
Alvar Aalto
1964

Aalto University Library ⌄ ⌐
Otaniementie 9, Espoo
Alvar Aalto
1970

In 1949 the Finnish Government purchased the site of the Otaniemi manor to build the new campus Helsinki's University of Technology. The main building of the university campus, located on a small hill, is the most prominent building there. The structure containing the auditorium is placed in the bend of the L-shaped building and forms an outdoor amphitheater. The seminar rooms are oriented towards small courtyards. The facades are characterized by red brick and black granite. In 2010, the university, was renamed in Alvar Aalto University in honor of its famous alumnus.

The library frames the main quadrangle on the campus of the University of Helsinki in Espoo. The architecture of the building, designed by Alvar Aalto, is designed to guarantee optimal working conditions for the students. Book storage is located in the three basement floors while the work desks and the book shelves are to be found in a faceted component to the side. The main rectangular volume contains offices and seminar rooms. In addition to the main building and the adjacent library, a shopping center and a water tower were also designed by Alvar alto.

Nokia Headquarters ⌄
Keilalahdentie 4, Espoo
Pekka Helin, Harri Koski
1997

L 150

The headquarters building of Finland's most famous company, Nokia, is located on the western highway at the eastern entrance to the city of Espoo in Keilaniemi and thus easily visible from and nearby to Helsinki. The 40,000 square feet building was designed by the two Finnish architects Pekka Helin and Harri Koski and was built between 1995 and 1997. The Nokia headquarters building is oriented towards Keilalahti Bay, which is also the first thing visitors see on entering the foyer of the main office complex. Approximately 1,200 people work in the building. The triangular office spaces are organized around two large atriums and a glazed gallery with suspended pedestrian bridges connects the two areas. Towards the entrance side, the Nokia headquarters building has eight floors, but towards the water-side the building only has five stories. The architecture of the building appears rather technical and cool because of its expression in the use of steel and glass as omnipresent construction materials. Particularly the buildings details are very fine: wooden floors and ceilings give warmth to the interior and also a friendly atmopshere. One atrium contains the cafeteria and the other houses meeting rooms. The headquarters building itself has a double facade protecting against external weather influences. It was extended in 2001 and it is well worth a visit.

Otaniemi Chapel
Jämeräntaival 8, Espoo
Kaija and Heikki Sirén
1957

L 151

Multi-Purpose Building
Kotkatie 4, Espoo
Matti Nurmela et al.
1987

152

The Otaniemi Chapel is a the high-point of Finnish architecture style from the Fifties. The ecclesiastical building has an altar wall which opens fully to the surrounding forest making the surrounding nature and the changing seasons the visual and spiritual heart of worship. Behind the glass wall a simple steel cross was placed in the garden. The covered atrium leads to the low entrance hall and on to the chapel for 180 worshipers with its pitched roof. The side walls and floors are made of brick, but the ceiling and roof are wooden. The chapel was rebuilt after a fire in 1978.

The Karakallio Multi-Purpose Building was constructed by the Finnish architects Nurmela Matti, Kari Raimoranta and Jykri Tasa. Situated on a hillside between the road and a sports field at the rear, the building with its red brick facade faces the street with a curved roof, which is interrupted in the middle by the skylight of the lobby. This skylight divides the rectangular building into two halves. A canopy protects the entrance. The large hall is used for concerts and theater performances. Rehearsal rooms, children's and youth facilities are also part of the program.

Dipoli Student Center ⌄   `L 153`
Otakaari 24, Espoo
Raila and Reima Pietilä
1966

School and Day Care Center ⌃   `154`
Hösmärinahde 5, Espoo
Yrjo Suonto
2005

The Student Center on the campus of the Alvar Aalto University called "Dipoli" (dipole) was among the first buildings after the decision to relocate the campus from the city to Otaniemi was made. Two Finnish architects Raili and Reima Pietilä won an architectural design competition for the "Dipoli" in 1961. Since 1993, the building is used as the university's educational center. It offers 20 conference rooms and a couple of auditoriums. In the unusually deep building, free-form circulation areas contrast with the rectangular spaces for the primary uses. The large dining hall above is connected to the adjacent foyer and an auditorium. The facades are made of concrete, copper strips and rough stone and the interior walls and floors are covered in wood.

The Hösmärinpuisto School and Day Care Center is a good example of ecological and multi-functional space. The structure is made entirely of wood. A garden courtyard is framed by the two-story wing and forms a safe playground for the children. The classrooms, recreation rooms and workshops are all seamlessly interconnected. A bridge made of wood and glass connects the school with a cafeteria and offices. At night the cafeteria, the gym and work spaces are used by the local residents. The sports hall can also double as an auditorium and can be connected with a cafeteria by means of sliding walls which, in summer, can be opened out to the schoolyard. Rainwater is collected and the building demonstrates the efficient use of solar energy.

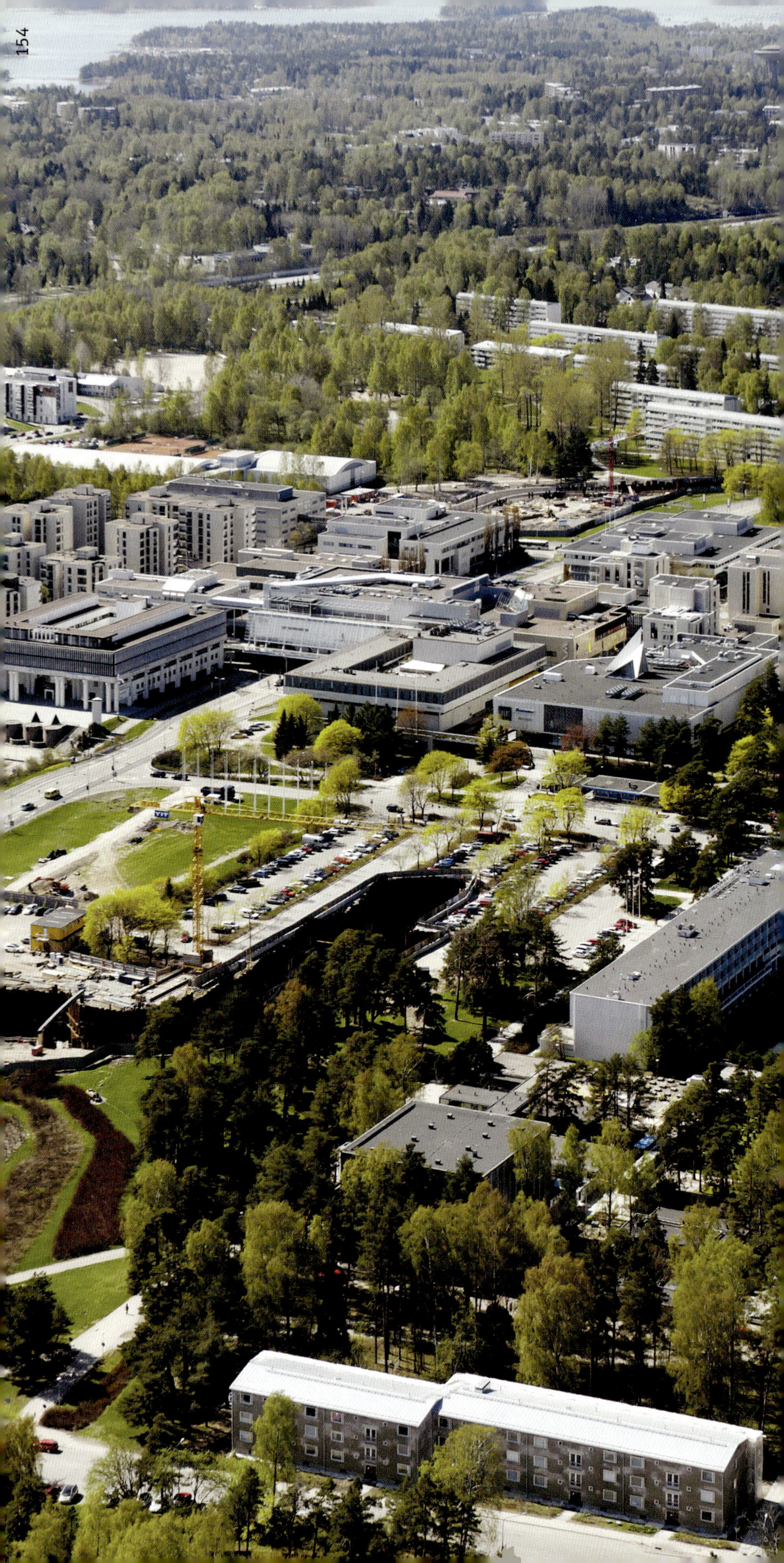

155

5

156

Tapiola Church
Kirkkopolku 4, Espoo
Aarno Ruusuvuori
1964

Tapiola Tower ≽
Tapiontori, Espoo
Aarne Ervi
1961

From the outside at first glance the church in Tapiola looks like an unattractive and Brutalist gray concrete cube. But precisely for that reason the brittle gray of the concrete walls makes the sparingly used, bright colors of the textiles and the ascetic details of the organ and the altar even more startling. Tall, closed concrete walls surround the chapel, which is lit from the back via a subdivided screen in the rear wall. Daylight penetrates the hall from above creating a mysterious play of light on the front wall. The low ancillary rooms are grouped around small courtyards; a wide corridor leads and connects them to the high cube. In 1992, an extension wing was added.

The Tapiola Tower ("Keskustorni") is the architectural emblem of the new town of Tapiola. Situated between the central basin ("Keskusallas") and the shopping center, the tower marks the heart of the city district. Designed by Aarne Ervi and completed in 1961, the tower has a height of 51 meters. The building itself is divided into three parts: a glass base with pilotis, eleven office floors above and a free-form capital called "Butterfly". In the meantime the rooftop restaurant has been converted into office spaces and the office walls are clad in enameled steel panels and are triple-loaded. When the tower is illuminated at night it shines in the artificial light and looks very similar to a lighthouse.

Helsinki-Vantaa Airport
Lentoasemantie, Vantaa
Keijo Ström et al.
1969, 1983, 1993, 2004, 2009

The Vantaa Airport in Helsinki was opened for the Olympic Games in 1952, when air traffic was moved here from Malmi Airport. The main building, now *Terminal 1*, was designed by Keijo Ström and Olavi Tuomisto and opened in 1969 (and expanded 1983). The airport facilities were was gradually supplemented by another terminal: In 1993, at acute angles to the main building a domestic flight terminal was built after a design by Kalevi Ruokosuo, Ralf Åkerblom and Aki Alanko. In 2004 *Terminal 2*, designed by Pekka Salminen, was expanded. The extension of *Terminal 2* is located between the old international terminal and the domestic terminal and forms a corner between the two flanks, which are at acute angles to each other. The building is constructed on a triangular geometry. The distinctive tower has the shape of an inverted cone on the ground floor and offers a vantage point. The roof of the departure hall consists of a curved, triangular space frame and rests on three pillar bundles that branch out like a tree at the top. The floor also has a triangular grid. In 2009 the terminal was expanded by Antero Kummu and Bratislav Toskovic (Parviainen Architects) to accommodate long haul flights to East Asia.

Heureka Science Center
Tiedepuisto 1, Vantaa
Heikkinen-Komonen-Architects
1989

M 158

The Science Center is 8,200 square meters in size and is located at the intersection of the main railway line in the country with the Kerava river. The collage-like design combines components of concrete, steel and wood and contains an auditorium, seminar rooms, a planetarium and a cinema. Each component has its own structure. Visitors can view different phenomena resulting from scientific experiments. Along the adjacent railway line the center has a glass facade with noise protection. The steel components show the color spectrum of light. In the center of the hall there is a large cylindrical building with a spoke-like roof structure.

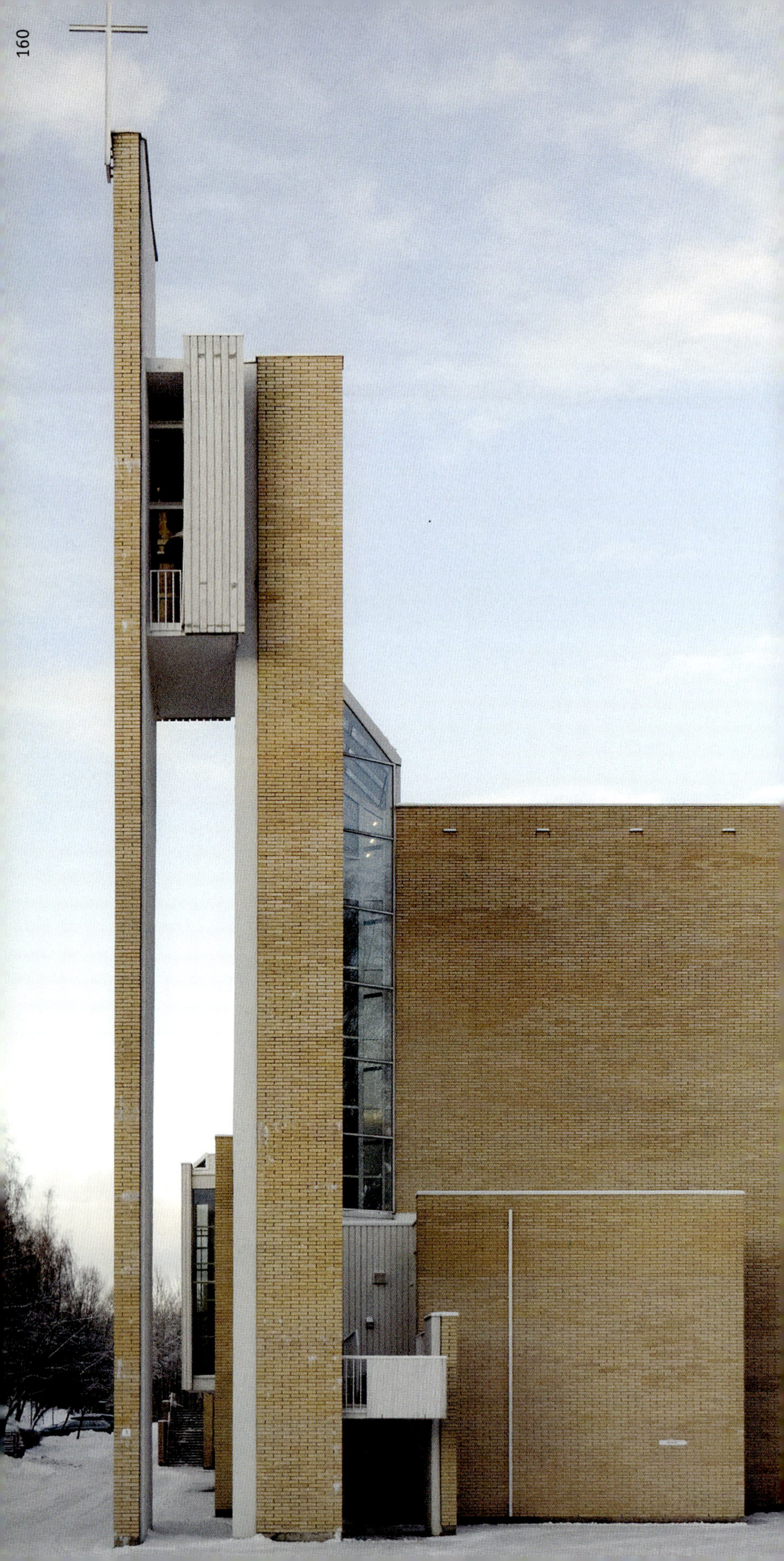

Myyrmäki Church   K 159
Uomatie 1, Vantaa
Juha Leiviskä
1984

St. Lawrence Chapel ⌃ ⌄   M 160
Pappilankuja 3, Vantaa
Avanto Architects
2010

The narrow Myyrmäki Church is located on an elongated plot of land adjacent to an elevated commuter rail link. It is considered one of the most successful religious buildings by Juha Leiviskä. A segmented wall of yellow bricks forms the backbone of the church towards the railway. Towards a small grove at the rear there are the longitudinal prayer hall, a chapel, two congregation halls and offices, children's and youth areas. The church resembles the vertical trunks of birch trees. The altar, which is naturally lit from the side, is placed along the long side, with the organ loft along the opposite. The hall with 460 seats is lit from above by a skylight. Visitors first enter via a low, dark lobby, after which the effect of the bright, light-filled rooms is all the more dramatic.

Avanto, a young architect's office, won an open design competition for the construction of a crematorium in 2003. The low chapel integrates various elements of the exterior space and does not compete visually with the medieval stone church nearby: the facades are made of masonry, natural stone, patinated copper and metallic fabrics. The design seeks to imbue the cremation ceremony with peace and dignity and the architects have indeed succeeded in complementing the transition from mortality to eternity architecturally. The walk through the building is tastefully and sensitively accentuated with a variety of lighting effects and spatial features while the courtyards act as passages for the ceremony; the mourners can look into the light or enjoy spatial enclosure.

162

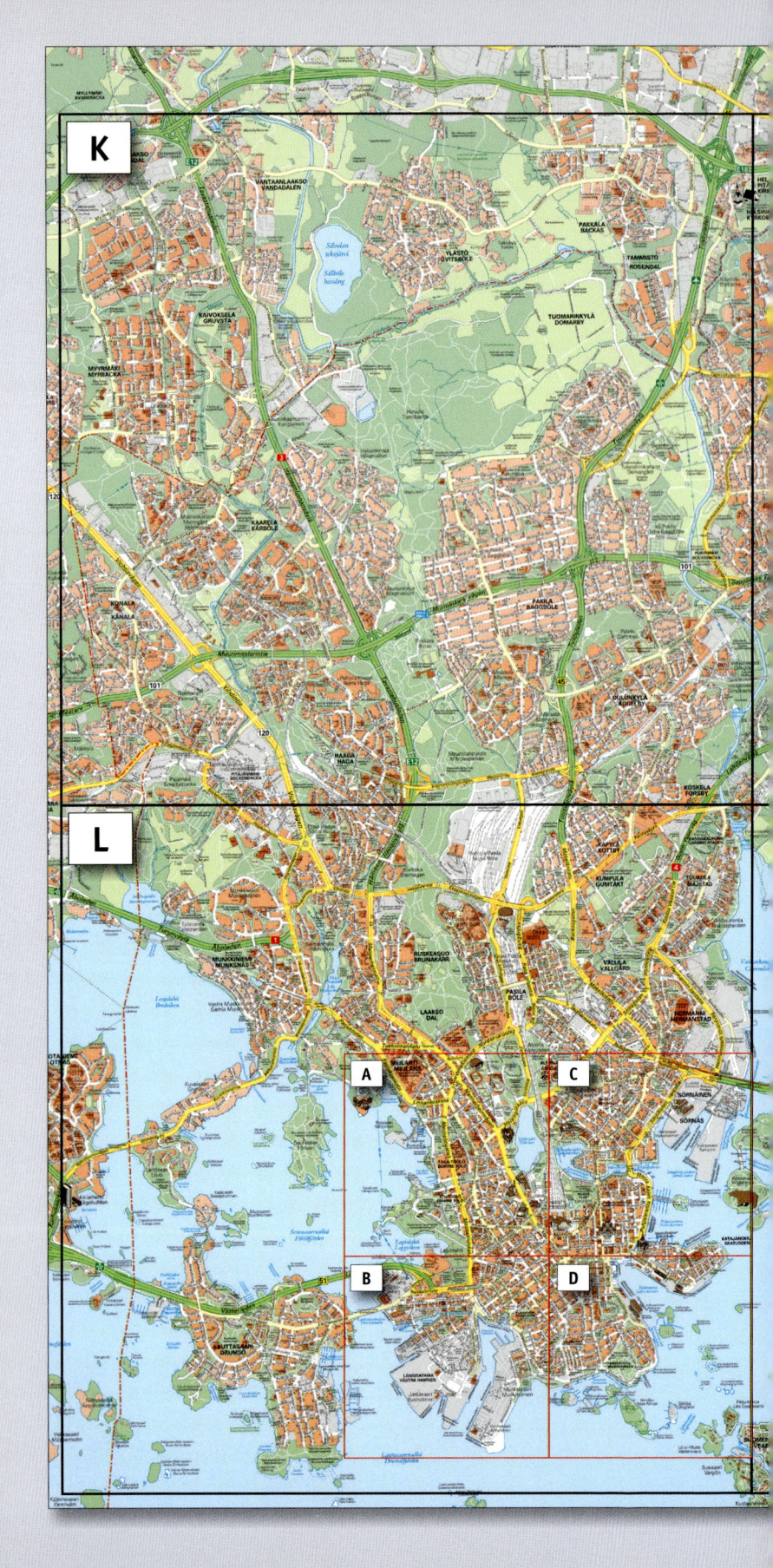

K

L

A C

B D

163

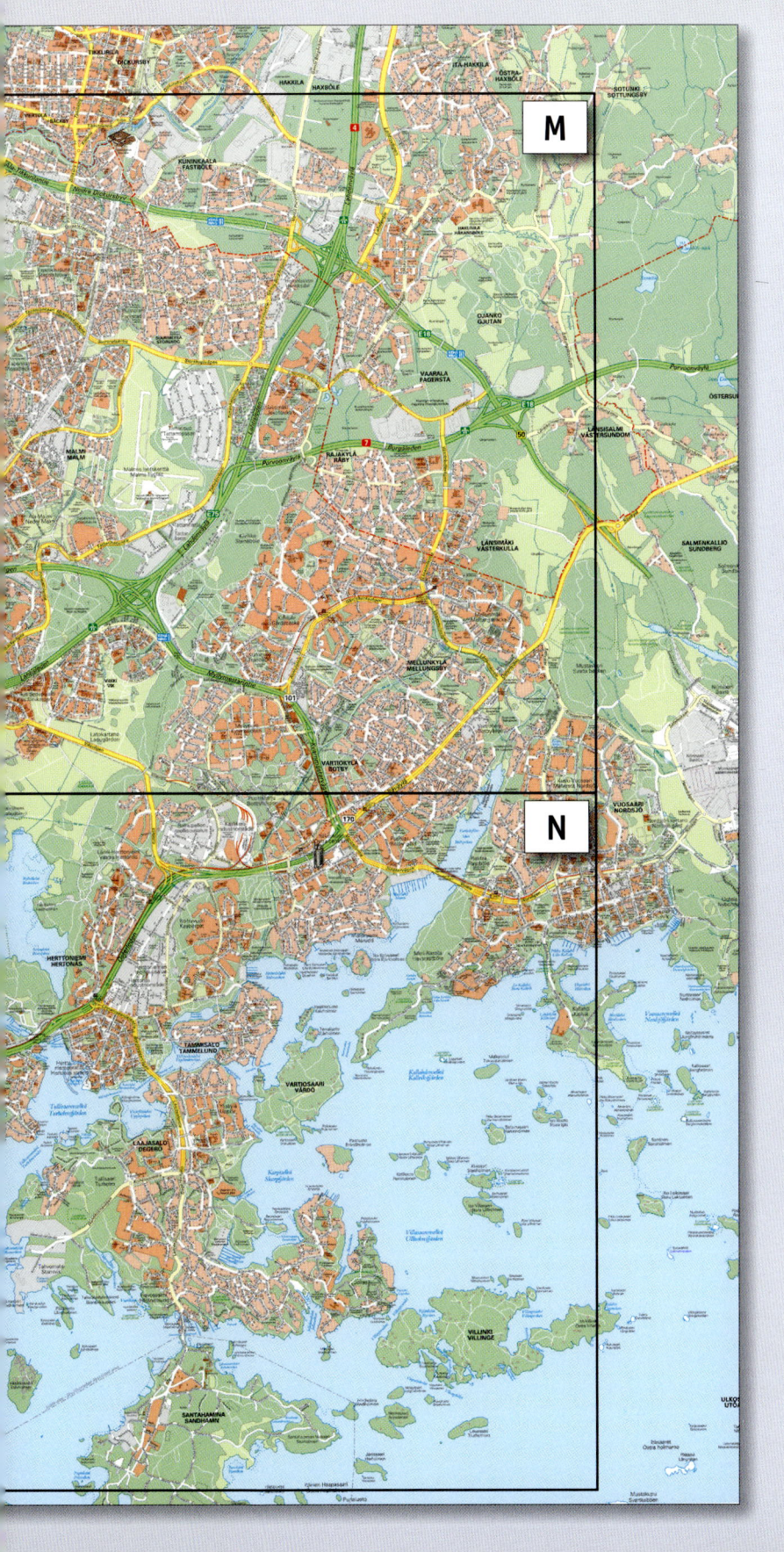

K
KEHÄ RING III
E12
VANTAANLAAKSO VANDADALEN
Tavastehusleden
Silvolan tekojärvi
Sillböle bassäng
Martinlaakso
Mårtensdalsvägen
Martinkyläntie
Vantaanlaaksontie
Vantaankoski Vandaforsen
Perkiö Nybolandet
Kivimäki Stenbacka
Louhela
159
KAIVOKSELA GRUVSTA
MYYRMÄKI MYRBACKA
Myyrmäki
Rajatorpantie
Vaskivuorentie
Kopparbergsv
Raappavuorentie
Honkasuo Hongasmossa
Kuninkaantammi Kungseken
Hämeenlinnanväylä
3
Malminkartano Malmgård
Malminkartano
KAARELA KÅRBÖLE
Vihdintie
Vichtisvägen
KONALA KÅNALA
Kannelmäki Gamlas
Kannelmäki
098
Muurimestarintie
101
Reimarla Reimars
Pohjois-Haaga Norra Haga
Lassila Lassas
Marttila Martas
120
Pitäjänmäentie
Pitäjänmäki
Teollisuuskatu
Mäkkylä
HAAGA HAGA
Mästarv
Painiitty Pajängen
Hakunila Håkansåker
Rajatorppa Råtorp
Kuninkaantammentie
Vantaa

165

PAKKALA / BACKAS
YLÄSTÖ / ÖVITSBÖLE
TAMMISTO / ROSENDAL
TUOMARINKYLÄ / DOMARBY
PAKILA / BAGGBÖLE
Länsi-Pakila / Västra Baggböle
Itä-Pakila / Östra Baggböle
PUKINMÄKI / BOCKSBACKA
OULUNKYLÄ / ÅGGELBY
Paloheinä / Svedängen
Torpparinmäki / Torparbacken
Tuomarinkartano / Domargård
Patola / Dammen
Pirkkola / Britas
Maunula / Månsas
Metsälä / Krämersskog

L
A
B
Pajamäki
Smedjebacka
Teollisuusalue
Industriområde
PITÄJÄNMÄKI
SOCKENBACKA
Sockenbackavägen
Pitäjänmäentie
Vihdintie
Vihtisvägen
Etelä-Haaga
Södra Haga
HAAGA
HAGA
Vermo
Tali
Iso Huopalahti
Stora Hoplaxviken
Munkkivuori
Munkshöjden
Talinranta
Talistranden
Lapinmäentie
Turunväylä
Åboleden
Mannerheimintie
Niemenmäki
Näshöjden
MUNKKINIEMI
MUNKSNÄS
Vanha Munkkiniemi
Gamla Munksnäs
Laajalahti
Bredviken
Huopalahdentie
Ramsaynranta
Paciusgatan
077
087
089
Kuusisaari
Granö
083
085
Kuusisaarentie
Seurasaari
Fölisön
086
Granövägen
Björnholmsvägen
Lehtisaari
Lövö
Kaskisaari
Svedjeholmen
Mustasaari
Svartholmen
Seurasaarenselkä
Fölisöfjärden
148
151
153
149
142
143
150
Keilalahti
Kägelviken
Hanasaari
Hanaholmen
Västerleden
51
Drumsövägen
Lauttasaarentie
LAUTTASAARI
DRUMSÖ
Vattuniemi
Hallonnäs
Niittysaaret
Ängsholmarna
Mäntysaari
Tallholmen
Pohjoinen Käärmeluoto
Norra Ormkobben
Läntinen Käärmeluoto
Västra Ormkobben
Itäinen Käärmeluoto
Östra Ormkobben
Käärmekari
Ormgrunden

Mäntsäparken
Krämertsskogsvägen
Metsäläntie
Asesepäntie
Tuusulanväylä
KOSKELA
FORSBY
KÄPYLÄ
KOTTBY
Forsbyvägen
090
Pohjois-Pasila
Norra Böle
KUMPULA
GUMTÄKT
VANHAKAUPUNKI
GAMMELSTADEN
136
4
TOUKOLA
MAJSTAD
103
100
Skogsbackavägen
Koskelantie
Mäkelänkatu
109
078
105
Itä-Pasila
Östra Böle
133
088
RUSKEASUO
BRUNAKÄRR
104
VALLILA
VALLGÅRD
Hämeentie
Kustaa Vaasan tie
Gustav Vasas väg
PASILA
BÖLE
LAAKSO
DAL
139
HERMANNI
HERMANSTAD
108
Hermannin rantatie
Teollisuuskatu
130
Nordenskiöldinkatu
Nordenskiöldsg
Alppila
Albyddan
ALPPIHARJU
ÅSHÖJDEN
C
Helsingegatan
KALLIO
BERGHALL
SÖRNÄINEN
SÖRNÄS
Sörnäisten rantatie
Helsinginkatu
Mannerheimintie
Mannerheimvägen
Töölönlahti
Tölöviken
Linjat
Linjerna
Hanasaari
Hanaholmen
Sompasaari
Sumparn
TAKA-TÖÖLÖ
BORTRE TÖÖLÖ
Mechelingatan
Mechelininkatu
ETU-TÖÖLÖ
FRÄMRE TÖÖLÖ
KLUUVI
GLOET
KRUUNUNHAKA
KRONOHAGEN
Tervasaari
Tjärholmen
Pohjoissatama
Norra hamnen
Pohjoisranta
Norra kajen
Arkadiankatu
Lapinniemi
Lappudden
Lapinlahti
Lappviken
Pohjoisesplanadi
KAMPPI
KAMPEN
D
KAARTINKAUPUNKI
Porkalankatu
Porkalag
Lönnrotinkatu
Eteläsatama
Södra hamnen
Valkosaari
Blekholmen
PUNAVUORI
RÖDBERGEN
ULLANLINNA
ULRIKASBORG
KAIVOPUISTO
BRUNNSPARKEN
Luoto
Klippan
Munkkisaari
Munkholmen
Harakka
Stora Räntan
Särkkä
Långören
Hernesaari
Hernesaari
Artholmen
Länsi-Musta
Västersvartö
Susisaari
Vargö

M
HELSINGIN PITÄJÄN KIRKONKYLÄ
HELSINGE KYRKOBY
160
VIERTOLA
BÄCKBY
158
50
Ala-Tikkurilantie
Nedre Dickursbyv
Tikkurilantie
Dickurv
Tuusulanväylä
Tusbyleden
Keravanjoki
SUUTARILA
SKOMAKARBÖLE
Skomakarbölevägen
Suutarilantie
Tapulikaupungintie
Stapelstadsvägen
Tapulikaupunki
Stapelstaden
Suuntimotie
Puistola
Parkstad
Siltamäki
Brobacka
Töyrynummi
Lidmalmen
Staffansbyvägen
Tapanilankaari
Mosabackabågen
Suurmetsäntie
Tapaninkyläntie
TAPANINKYLÄ
STAFFANSBY
094
Tapanila
Mosabacka
Malminkaari
Staffans-slättsvägen
Tapaninvainio
Staffansslätten
Malmbågen
123
MALMI
MALM
106
Malmin lentok
Malms flyg
Ylä-Malmi
Övre Malm
095
Bocksbackavägen
Tapanivaiontie
Ala-Malmi
Nedre Malm
Sepänmäki
Smedsbacka
Tattariharjuntie
PUKINMÄKI
BOCKSBACKA
Pukinmäenkaari
Seppämestarintie
Smedsmästarsvägen
Pihlajamäki
Rönnbacka
Pihlajamäentie
Malmin hautausmaa
Malms kyrkogård
Savela
Lerstrand
Pihlajisto
Rönninge
Veräjälaakso
Grinddal
Veräjämäki
Grindbacka
Rönnbackavägen
Lahtisleden
110
138
115
135
VIIKKI
VIK
Viikin tiedepuisto
Viks forskarpark
116
Viikinmäki
Viksbacka
Viikintie
Viksvägen
Latokartano
Ladugården
Vanhankaupunginkoski

Lahdenväylä
Lahdentie
Lahtisvägen
Vanha Porvoontie
Gamla Borgåvägen
Jokiniementie
Anäsvägen
Håkansbölevägen
KEHÄ RING III
HAKUNILA
HÅKANSBÖLE
Heikinlaakso
Henriksdal
Heikinlaaksontie
E18
E75
VAARALA
FAGERSTA
OJANKO
GJUTAN
Fazerintie
Fazersvägen
Lahtisleden
Jakomäki
Jakobacka
Tattarisuontie
Porvoonväylä
Borgåleden
RAJAKYLÄ
RÅBY
Maratontie
Maratonvägen
Västerkullavägen
Kivikko
Stensböle
Vesala
Arvings
LÄNSI
VÄSTER
Kontula
Gårdsbacka
Kurkimäki
Tranbacka
MELLUNKYLÄ
MELLUNGSBY
Mellunmäki
Mellungsbacka
Länsimäentie
Myllymestarintie
Kontulantie
Myllypuro
Kvarnbacken
Vartioharju
Botbyåsen
4
7
101
113
126

N
Vikksstranden
Hakalanniemi
Hakalaudden
Ruohokarinniemi
Gräsörsudden
Luonnonsuojelualue
Naturskyddsområde
Loppi
Klobben
Lammassaari
Fårholmen
Kokkoluoto
Kuusiluoto
Granholmen
Arabianranta
Arabiastranden
Ryönälahti
Brakviken
Fastholma
Fastholmen
Länsi-Herttoniemi
Västra Hertonäs
Vanhankaupunginselkä
Gammelstadsfjärden
Saunalahti
Bastuviken
HERTTONIEMI
HERTONÄS
Österleden
Herttoniemen teollisuusalue
Hertonäs industriområde
Byläsaari
Byholmen
Kivinokka
Stenudden
Varjosaari
Skuggan
Leposaari
Vilan
Verkkosaari
Nätholmen
KULOSAARI
BRÄNDÖ
Itäväylä
170
Raitalahti
Pilviken
Herttoniemenranta
Hertonäs strand
Linnanrakentajantie
Borgbyggarvägen
Hermanstads strandväg
107
Hopeasalmi
Silversundet
Tullisaarenselkä
Turholmsfjärden
Ylisküläntahti
Uppbyviken
Killingholma
Killingholmen
Mustikkamaa
Blåbärslandet
MUSTIKKAMAA-
KORKEASAARI
BLÅBÄRSLANDET-
HÖGHOLMEN
Sompasaari
Sumparn
Korkeasaari
Högholmen
Palosaari
Paloholmen
Hylkysaari
Vrakholmen
Tullisaarensalmi
Turholmssundet
LAAJASALO
DEGERÖ
Tullisaari
Turholm
Koirasaarentie
Kaitalahti
Hålvik
Hundholmsvägen
KATAJANOKKA
SKATUDDEN
Haakoninlahti
Håkansviken
Tahvonlahti
Stansvik
Koirasaari
Hundholmen
Pitkäluoto
Långholmen
Tahvonlahdenniemi
Stansviksudden
Hevossalmi
Hästnässund
Kruunuvuorenselkä
Kronbergsfjärden
Koivusaari
Björkholmen
Lonna
Lonnan
Vasikkasaari
Kalvholmen
Suoja-alue - Skyddsområde Restricted area
Pikku-Musta
Lilla Östersvartö
Iso Mustasaari
Stora Östersvartö

Puotinharju
Botbyhöjden
Kasåkers
industriområde
Itäkeskus
Östra centrum
170
134
111
125
127
137
112
114
Meripellontie
Sjöåkervägen
Vuotie
Puotila
Botby gård
Vartiokylänlahti
Botbyviken
Rastila
Rastböle
Marjaniemi
Marudd
Meri-Rastila
Havsrastböle
Iso Koivusaari
Stora Björkholmen
Strömsinlahti
Strömsviken
Vasikkaluoto
Kalvholmen
Tervaluoto
Tjärholmen
Kortlahti
Korsvik
Ramsinniemi
Ramsöudden
Härkäsaari
Tjurholmen
VARTIOSAARI
VÅRDÖ
Kallahdenselkä
Kallviksfjärden
Malkasaari
Takvedaholmen
MISALO
ELUND
Yliskylä
Uppby
Poikasaari
Pojkholmen
Paloluoto
Brändholmen
Pohjoinen Villaluoto
Norra Ullholmen
Läntinen Villaluoto
Västra Ullholmen
Itäinen Villaluoto
Östra Ullholmen
Kotiluoto
Hemholmen
Kivisaari
Stenholmen
Karpiselkä
Skarpfjärden
Puuskaniemi
Knysnäs
Teerikaislikko
Orrvassen
Repossaari
Repoxholmen
Aittasaari
Bodholmen
Iso Villasaari
Stora Ullholmen
Villasaarenselkä
Ullholmsfjärden
Poikaluodot
Pojkholmarna
Jollas
Jollaksentie
Jollasvägen
Maunumkari
Månsholmen
Kylänlahti
Byviken
VILLINKI
VILLINGE
Lehmäsaari
Koholmen
Matosaari
Maskholmen
Pukkiluoto
Bockholmen
Viipurinkaita
Viborgsgattet
Neitsytsaari
Jungfruholmen
Kuusiluoto
Granholmen
Hintholma
Hindholmen
Hernesaari
Artholmen
AHAMINA
DHAMN
Louesaari

Architects
Digits indicate the project numbers.

Aalto, Alvar 002, 003, 006, 008, 014, 037, 042, 061, 077, 084, 102, 148, 149
A6 Architects 034
Akerblom, Ralf 157
Alanko, Aki 157
AMFI Architects 100
Anttinen Oiva Architects 052
ARK-house Architects 115, 126, 136
Armanto, Mikko 078
Auttila, Pieta-Linda 048
Avanto Architects 140, 160
Baeckmann, Woldemar 057, 071
Beckmann N'Thépé 141
Bjöland, Svein 041
Björklund, Asta 108
Blomstedt, Pauli E. 015
Castrén-Jauhiainen-Nuuttila 142
Castrén, Heikki 007
Castrén, Jalmari 031
CJN Architects 104
Davidsson, Aki 053
Dinkha Latchin Associates 107
Ekelund, Hilding 068, 072, 080, 105
Eklund, Jarl 068
Englund, Dag 106
Erholtz, Markku 135
Ervi, Aarne 005, 079, 145, 156
Frosterus, Sigurd 012
Grebenshtshikov, E. S. 043
Grut, Torben 030
Gullichsen, Kairamo & Vormala 011, 013
Gullichsen, Kristian 093, 123
Häkli, Seppo 086, 094
Harmia, Hugo 071, 072
Haukkavaara, Jyri 034
Heikkinen-Komonen-Architects 158
Heikkinen, Mikko 089, 117
Helin, Pekka 039, 060, 064, 146, 150
HKP Architects 046, 050, 062
Holl, Steven 054
Huttunen, Erkki 020, 130
Huttunen, Hannu 135
Hytönen, Aarne 027, 082
Hyvärinen, Kari 047
Ijäs, Jouni 129
Ilonen, Arvi and Pirkko 103, 112
Jäntti, Toivo 097, 099
Järvi, Jorma 017
Järvinen, Kari 114
JKMM Architects 110
Jokela, Olli-Pekka 023, 091
Jung & Jung 040
K2S Architects 018
Kairamo, Erkki 137
Kallio, Oiva 036
Karhunen, Jukka 134
Karjalainen, Jussi 135
Kentala, Janne 117
Kokko, Niilo 024
Kokkola-Lemarchand, Ritva 101
Kommonen, Marku 117
Koski, Harri 150
Krakström, Erik 032
Krogius, Björn 111
Kuismanen, Kimmo 116
Kummu, Antero 157
Kumon, Marko 089
Lahdelma & Mahlamäki 090, 109, 138
Lahdelma, Ilmari 095
Lehtinen, Armas and Pauli 045
Lehtinen, Ilona 047
Leiviskä, Juha 069, 076, 085, 096, 108, 159
Lemarchand, Olivier 101
Leppänen, Kaarlo 047, 133
Lindegren, Yrjö 035, 097
Lindroos, Erik 017, 103
Löfström, Kaarina 132
LPR Architects 059, 063
Lundström, Helge 009
Luukkonen, Risto-Veikko 027, 082
Mahlamäki, Rainer 127
Mäkinen, Heikki 125
Mäkinen, Matti 132
Malmström, Karl 103
Martikainen, Martta 081
Nieminen, Merja 114
Nurmela, Matti 152
Paatela, Jussi 021
Paatela, Jussi and Toivo 033
Paatela, Toivo 120
Paavilainen, Käpy and Simo 083, 113
Pallasmaa, Juhani 019
Palmqvist, Wäinö Gustaf 056
Parviainen Architects 157
Penttilä, Timo 128, 129
Petäjä, Keijo 022
Pietilä, Raila and Reima 153
Pöyry Architects 075
Quinlan, Steven 044
Raimoranta, Kari 131, 152
Retzius, Eyvind 041

Revell, Viljo 007, 022, 031, 083, 092
Rosendahl, Vera 072, 106
Ruokosuo, Kalevi 157
Ruusuvuori, Aarno 029, 147, 155
Saarela, Heikki 129
Saarinen, Eliel 001, 004, 087
Salminen, Pekka 157
Salonen, Kati 134
SARC 139, 143
Siikala, Antti-Matti 055, 143
Siitonen, Tuomo 065, 066, 073, 074
Simberg, Kurt 070
Sipari, Osmo 092, 098
Sipinen, Arto 144
Siren, Heikki and Kaija 051, 124, 151
Sirén, Johan Sigfrid 028, 058
Söderlund, Jan 047

Sonck, Lars 010, 049, 121
Ström, Keijo 157
Suihkonen, Jaakko 047
Suomalainen, Timo and Tuomo 067
Suonto, Yrjö 154
Tasa, Jykri 131, 152
Taucher, Gunnar 016, 025
Tommila, Mauri 132
Toskovic, Bratislav 157
Tuomisto, Olavi 157
Ullberg, Uno 026
Vähäkallio, Väinö 074, 118, 119, 122
Valjakka, Ilmo 088
Valkama, Esko 065, 066
Verhe, Peter 039
Vormala, Timo 093

Directory
Digits indicate the project numbers.

Helsinki

Agronominkatu 5: 110
Aleksanterinkatu 17: 015
Aleksanterinkatu 52b: 012
Areenankuja 1: 100
Arkadiankatu 3: 060
Aurorankatu 6: 059
Bulevardi 42: 057
Centralgatan: 013
Eläintarhantie 5: 128
Elimäenkatu 5: 139
Emännänpolku 1: 113
Energiakatu: 072
Eteläesplanadi 14: 014
Eteläesplanadi 18: 028
Eteläesplanadi 22: 026
Eteläranta 10: 022
Fabianinkatu 26: 053
Fabianinkatu 29: 008
Fredrikinkatu 33: 045
Haartmaninkatu 4: 091
Haartmaninkatu 8: 093
Hämeentie 2: 121
Hämeentie 19: 122
Hämeentie 135a: 103
Helsinginkatu 56: 076
Helsinginkatu 58: 062
Hietakummuntie 19: 131
Hollantilaisentie 11: 087
Itäinen puistotie 17: 044
Itäkatu 1-7: 125

Itämerenkatu 11-13: 065
Itämerentori 2: 064
Itämerentori 9: 066
Jalavatie 6: 092
Kaarelankuja 2: 098
Kaikukatu 2: 118
Kaisaniemenkatu 5: 052
Kaisaniemenkatu 6: 036
Kaisaniemenkatu 13: 035
Kaisankuja: 051
Kaivokatu 6: 007
Kampinkuja 2: 006
Kanavakatu 4: 023
Kanavakatu 6: 010
Kanavaranta 1: 042
Kasarmikatu 24: 031
Katajanokanlaituri 6: 011
Katajanokanlaituri 8: 025
Kauppakartanonkatu 7: 137
Kenttäpolku 3: 095
Keskuskatu 1b: 004
Keskuskatu 3: 002
Kevätkatu 2: 135
Krogiuksentie 4: 085
Kunnantie 1: 123
Kuusilahdenkuja 1: 083
Laivastokatu 22: 032
Lars Sonckin tie 2: 107
Lintulahdenkatu 10: 119
Lintulahdenkuja 4: 117
Lutherinkatu 3: 067
Mäkelänkatu 70: 105

Malminrinne 6: 016
Mannerheiminaukio 2: 054
Mannerheimintie 9: 020
Mannerheimintie 11: 017
Mannerheimintie 13a: 063
Mannerheimintie 13e: 061
Mannerheimintie 20: 047
Mannerheimintie 22: 024
Mannerheimintie 302: 058
Marjaniementie 74: 127
Mechelininkatu 23: 081
Meritullinkatu 8: 039
Muotoilijankatu 3: 136
Mustialankatu 3: 138
Mustikkamaanpolku 12: 140, 141
Narinkka Square: 018
Nervanderinkatu 3: 068
Nordenskiöldinkatu 12: 084
Olavinlinnantie 6: 134
Olympiaranta 1: 027
Paavo Nurmen kuja 1c: 082
Paavo Nurmen tie 1: 097, 099
Paciuksenkatu 29: 089
Päijänteentie 3-5: 108
Palosuontie 1: 096
Parrukatu 1: 129
Pohjoisesplanadi 9: 030
Pohjoisesplanadi 11-13: 029
Pohjoisesplanadi 39: 003
Porkkalankatu 13: 074
Postintaival 7: 090
Provianttikatu 4: 126
Radiokatu 5: 088
Rajatie 7: 094
Ratakatu 9: 037
Ratapihantie 6: 104
Rautatieläisenkatu 8: 133
Rautatientori: 001
Rehbinderintie 17: 041
Reposalmentie 13: 114
Runeberginkatu 10: 070
Runeberginkatu 14: 071
Salmisaarenranta 11: 073
Salomonkatu 15: 009
Sandelsinkatu 3: 069
Satamakatu 3: 120
Satamasaarentie 7: 112
Seurasaari Museum Island: 086
Siltasaarenkatu 18: 124
Siltavuorenpenger 3a: 033
Siltavuorenpenger 5a: 034
Simonkatu 9: 050
Sörnäisten rantatie 23: 132
Sturenkatu 4: 102
Sturenkatu 17: 130

Tallberginkatu 1c: 056
Tammasaarenkatu 1-7: 075
Tattariharjuntie: 106
Tehtaankatu 1b: 043
Tehtaankatu 23: 049
Tiilimäki 20: 077
Töölönlahdenkatu 2: 055
Topeliuksenkatu 4: 080
Topeliuksenkatu 6: 079
Turunlinnantie 1-3: 111
Unioninkatu 39: 038
Unioninkatu 40: 021
Urheilukatu 1: 101
Urho Kekkosen katu 5b: 019
Uutiskatu: 078
Vaino Auerin Katu 11: 109
Valkosaari Island: 048
Viikkinkaari 2a: 116
Viikkinkaari 11a: 115
Yliopistokatu 3: 005
Yrjönkatu 26: 040

Espoo

Ahertajantie 5: 147
Hösmärinahde 5: 154
Jämeräntaival 8: 151
Kaupinkalliontie 10: 144
Keilalahdentie 4: 150
Keilaniementie 1: 142
Keilasatama 3: 143
Kirkkopolku 3: 145
Kirkkopolku 4: 155
Kotkatie 4: 152
Otakaari 1: 148
Otakaari 24: 153
Otaniementie 9: 149
Tapiontori: 156
Tuulikuja: 146

Vantaa

Lentoasemantie: 157
Pappilankuja 3: 160
Tiedepuisto 1: 158
Uomatie 1: 159

Authors

Ulf Meyer, born in 1970, studied at the Berlin Technical University and the Illinois Institute of Technology in Chicago. 2008–2010 Assistant Professor for sustainable urban design at Kansas State University in Manhattan/Kansas. 2010–2011 Hyde Chair of Excellence at the UNL (University of Nebraska-Lincoln). Lectures at universities and cultural centers in Europe, USA and Canada as well as Japan, China, Singapore, Australia, Malaysia, the Philippines and Taiwan. Author and editor of several publications on contemporary architecture.

Laura Kolbe, born in 1957, Professor of European History at the University of Helsinki. Laura Kolbe is a well known public and media figure in Finland, with research interests in urban, cultural and social history. She is active in many cultural organizations and municipal institutions, as well as on nationalcommittees and academic societies.

Heikki Mäntymäki, born in 1970, is a head of Helsinki City Planning department's communication unit which takes care of the department's media relations, public participation and marketing. Heikki Mäntymäki has written and edited several articles and produced many exhibitions about the future of Helsinki.

Douglas Gordon, born in 1951, studied at the Bartlett, UCL. He is an architect and spatial planner and has worked for the Greater London Council and the London Borough of Camden. Since coming to Finland he worked as chief architect for the Housing Fund of Finland during the Nineties and has specialized in putting together the Helsinki City's Development Plan and its Spatial Strategies for the city region.

The *Deutsche Nationalbibliothek* lists this publication in the *Deutsche Nationalbibliografie*; detailed bibliograpic data are available in the internet at http://dnb.d-nb.de.

ISBN 978-3-86922-212-7

A DOM publishers

© 2012 by DOM publishers, Berlin
www.dom-publishers.com

This work is subject to copyright. All rights are reserved, whether the whole part of the material is concerned, specifically the rights of translation, reprinting, recitation, broadcasting, reproduction on microfilms or in other ways, and storage or processing in data bases. Sources and copyright owners are given to the best of our knowledge. Please inform us of any we may have inadvertently omitted. We will endeavour to include them in any further edition.

Translation
Ulf Meyer

Final editing
Stefanie Villgratter

Final proofreading
Mariangela Palazzi-Williams
MPW Translations and Publishing Services

Design
Dominik Schendel

QR Codes
Christoph Gößmann

Maps
City Survey Division, Helsinki 061/2012

Printing
Tiger Printing Hong Kong, Co. Ltd., Shenzhen/China

Photo Credits

Derics, Dainis: 111 b; Eberle, Martin: 35, 58 tr/b, 59 t, 60b, 65 br, 71 b, 93 b, 100 b, 101 b, 103 b, 109 b, 110 b, 113, 116, 117 b, 118, 119, 134 t, 135 b, 138 tl, 143 tl, 145 t, 148, 149, 150 b, 151, 152, 153 b, 156, 157 t, 160, 161 tl; Fedchenko, Albert: 74 b; Halas, Antonin: 26 l, 42; Helsingi Kaupunki/Press Service: 6/7 b, 16, 17, 19–25 t, 26 r, 29, 38 t; iStockphoto: 72 b (harryfn), 73 (stocksnapper); Mäkelä, Joel/Tietoa Visualisointi: 6/7 t; Mark, Oleksiy: 18; Meuser, Philipp: 4 b, 5 t/c, 27 t/b, 28, 30–32, 34, 36, 37, 39 t, 40 b, 41, 44, 45 b, 46 b, 47 b, 51 b, 54, 55 b, 56, 57 b, 59 b, 61, 62 r, 65 bl, 68 l, 69 b, 75, 80, 81, 86–88, 89 b, 91 c/b, 94 t/bl, 95 b, 99 t, 104, 107 b, 110 t, 111 t, 112, 114 t, 115, 120, 123 b, 125–127 t, 129 b, 132, 133 b, 135 t, 136, 137 t, 138 b, 139 t, 140, 142 c/b, 144, 145 b, 150 t, 158/159 b; Meyer, Ulf: 70, 91 t, 92, 93 t, 124, 131, 137 b, 139 tl; Niemelä, Voitto: 142 b, 148 b; Pyynönen, Katri: 69 t, 76; Sadura, Henryk: 72 t; Sarica, Murat: 82; Savvateeva, Tatiana: 51 t, 83 b; Siebert, Holger: 33, 38 b, 40 t, 43 b, 45 t, 46 t, 48, 49, 50, 52, 53, 55 t, 58 tl, 63, 67, 84, 85, 89 t, 94 br, 95 t, 99 b, 105, 106 b, 109 t, 117 t, 127 b, 128 b, 129 t, 130, 131 b, 138 tr, 161 tr/b; Uusheimo, Tuomas: 27 c, 64, 65 t; Vallas, Hannu: 25 b, 146/147, 154/155; Valter, Vika: 128 t; Williams, Paul: 77. Not listed images courtesy of the architects or of the City of Helsinki/Press Department.